Drop Two Voicings Uncovered - Volume 1

Ged Brockie

Copyright © 2016 GMI - Guitar & Music Institute

www.guitarandmusicinstitute.com

ISBN 978-0-9955088-0-4

First published in Great Britain in 2016 by GMI - Guitar & Music Institute

Cover (illustration) by Ged Brockie

Printed in the United Kingdom

TABLE OF CONTENTS

A WORD FROM THE AUTHOR

This book is aimed at guitarists who have progressed beyond the beginner stage and are looking to learn to play chords over the entire guitar fretboard effectively and within meaningful chord progressions.

This book can be used on its own, or ideally, with the accompanying Youtube videos and backing tracks which are offered from the GMI - Guitar & Music Institute website. You will find further additional chord ideas on the GMI website which complement the ideas and concepts found within the pages that follow. The web address where you can download this extra material is detailed on page six and in the appendices at the back of this book.

I wanted to create a way of learning that was both easy to understand and use and which was accessible to as many people as possible. That is why the chords are presented in the "guitar box" format which most people will be familiar with.

I also wanted to keep the amount of text within the book to a bare minimum. Theoretical explanations and harmonic concepts are presented within the videos which accompany the lessons which are found on the GMI Youtube channel. I really would urge all of you who have a broadband connection to study the ideas presented here in conjunction with the videos created for this book. This approach will really help you understand the thinking behind these chordal voicings and their many applications.

The chords presented in "Drop Two Voicings Uncovered" encompass four adjacent strings and strictly adhere to this concept throughout. I have deliberately limited my attention to this approach to help create uniformity within the chordal structures which are then generated across several string sets.

Drop Two Voicings Uncovered is the realisation of many hours teaching students as well as my own study and performance. Many of my students did not initially know that they already played drop two voicings or the potential power these chord forms possess.

I hope that with the way in which this book and the other resources are structured you make fast and focused progress on the instrument that I fell in love with so many years ago.

Best Wishes Ged Brockie

Ged Brockie has performed in almost every conceivable musical scenario over a thirty year period. His own band recordings comprise his own compositions, arrangements and performance with some of Scotland's finest musicians (The Mirror's Image - Circular Records 2009, The Last View From Mary's Place - Circular Records 2004). He was one of the main writers in the Scottish Guitar Quartet (SGQ) recording three albums (Near The Circle 2001, Fait Accompli 2003, Landmarks 2005) touring across Europe to critical acclaim. The DVD "Five Innovations For Guitar & Orchestra - Circular Records 2011" featured Ged with a twenty one piece orchestra. He has also worked with the RSNO, OSO, Carl Davis, Hummie Mann, West End shows on tour, TV & radio, music industry events, all levels of music education from high school to university and has a wide range of compositions used in film, TV and media.

Ged is the lead instructor and driving force behind GMI and guides the programs of learning within it.

www.gedbrockie.com

UNDERSTANDING THE CHORD LEGEND

Although understanding the chords will be straightforward, here is a short guide just in case.

A couple of points:

1. The "inferred root" means that the root is not found or played within the chord, but this is where it is located for identification purposes.

2. The (n) which can be found in the minor section refers to "natural seventh" tone.

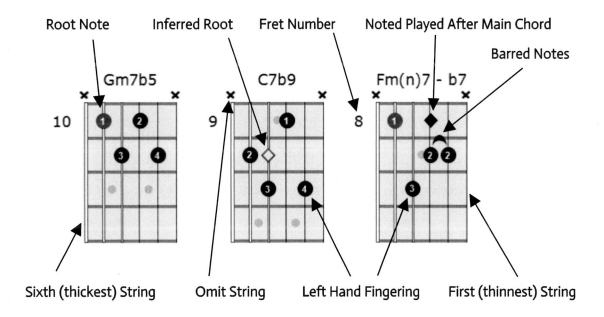

QR CODES FOR VIDEO ON YOUR PHONE OR TABLET!

The above image is a QR code. You will see these on every lesson introduction page where a video has been created to accompany it. These have been provided so you don't have to turn on a computer or want to quickly watch the relevant video on your mobile phone or tablet whilst at your music stand.

1. Download a QR code reader from Google Play or the Mac store. There are many free programs.

2. Once downloaded, open up the app and point at the QR code. The relevant video will then open.

HAVE YOU DOWNLOADED YOUR SUPPLEMENTARY MATERIAL YET?

1. Book owners should access all the additional learning material and backing tracks by going to the following web page...

   http://www.guitarandmusicinstitute/downloaddrop2voicings

2. For security purposes and in an effort to try and keep piracy to a bearable level you will be asked three questions which relate to words found on pages within this book. You will also be asked for your name and email.

3. A compressed file containing all the additional learning materials will be downloadable from a link contained within an email that will be sent to the email address you have stipulated on correct completion of the questions.

4. Make sure to check your spam folder regarding this email just incase nothing turn up within five to ten minutes.

5. Thank you for purchasing this book and supporting further publications from GMI, we really do appreciate it.

SECTION ONE

LEARNING THE BASIC CHORD FORMS

Lesson 1

Minor Seventh, Dominant Seventh, Major seventh Voicings
With Root & Melody Defined

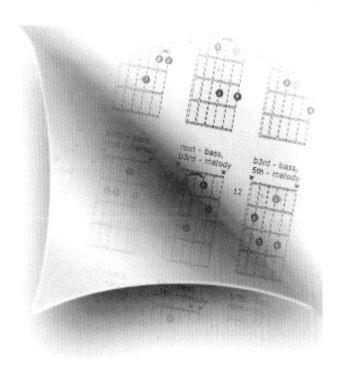

NOTES ABOUT LESSON 1

Drop 2 Voicings Uncovered Lesson 1 - Introduction to guitar drop two chords

In lesson one you will learn minor seventh, dominant seventh and major seventh chord forms. Each chord voicing is offered on three different string sets: 1 - 4, 2 - 5 and 3 - 6.

For each of the three chord types presented in the pages that follow, the chords found on any one string set have exactly the same note order as chords found on any other string set. Memorise the note relationships of the melody and bass to the chord as outlined in the diagrams. This will help you identify each chord across the fretboard.

YOUTUBE VIDEO

View the video that accompanies Lessons 1 on Youtube titled "Introduction To Guitar Drop Two Chords" at the following URL: www.youtube.com/watch?v=gPHc5MUG8sw

G minor 7 forms

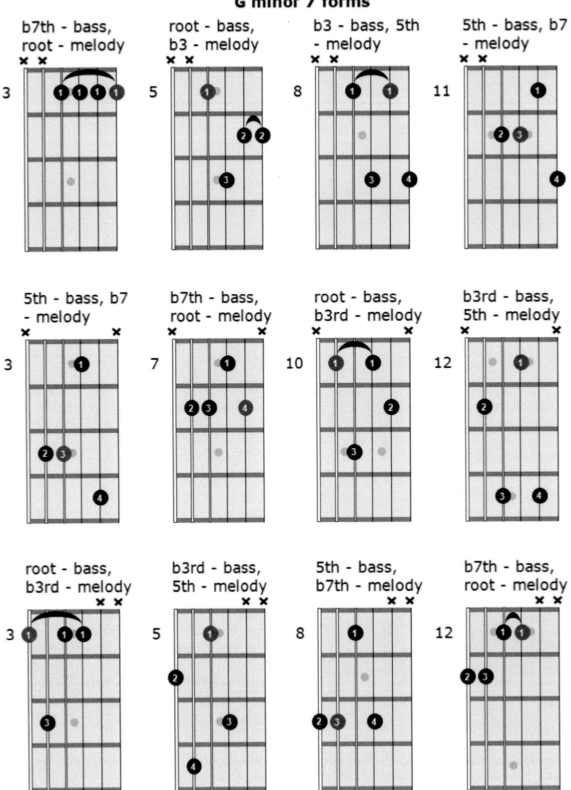

C7 forms

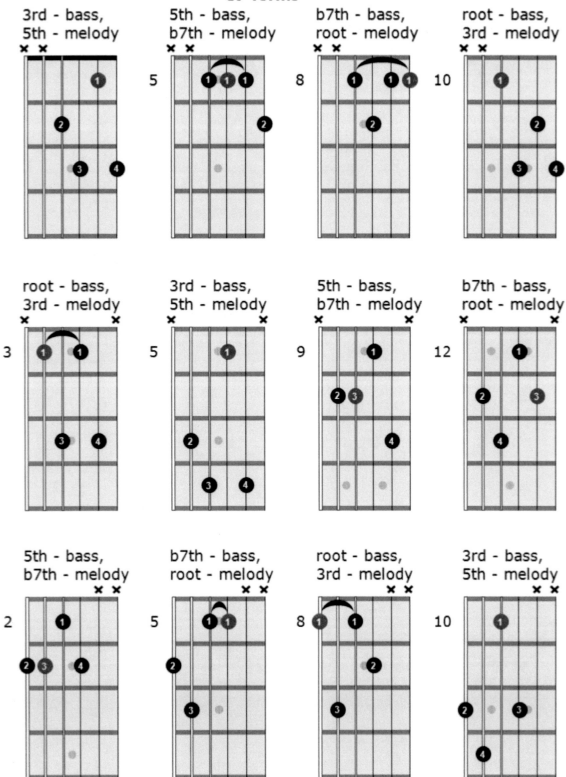

F Major seventh forms

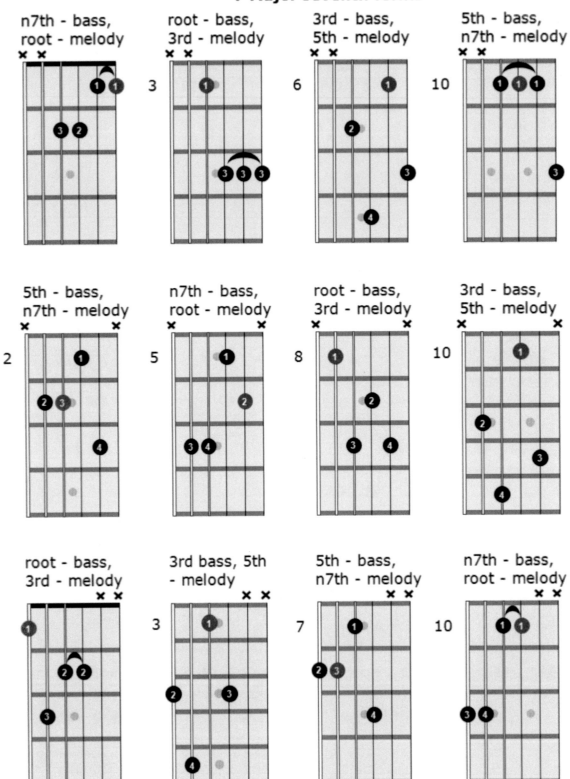

Lesson 2

Minor Seventh Chords Over All Three String Sets

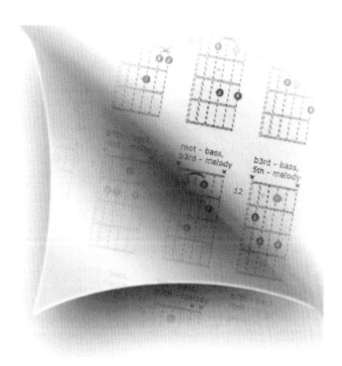

NOTES ABOUT LESSON 2

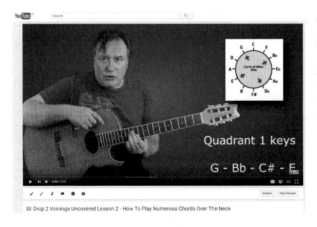

This lesson will really help you to learn the minor seventh chord voicings. Each string set offers four different minor seventh chords played up or down the neck in four key centres. Continue to learn other key centres not shown here for full understanding.

Use backing track 1 for Lesson 2.

YOUTUBE VIDEO

You can view the video "How To Play Numerous Chords Over The Neck" that accompanies Lessons 2, 3 and 4. The video includes theoretical concepts about these chords and how they were created across the neck.

View the video on Youtube at URL: www.youtube.com/watch?v=MQtSvZ2IjwQ

Minor Seventh String Set 1 - 4

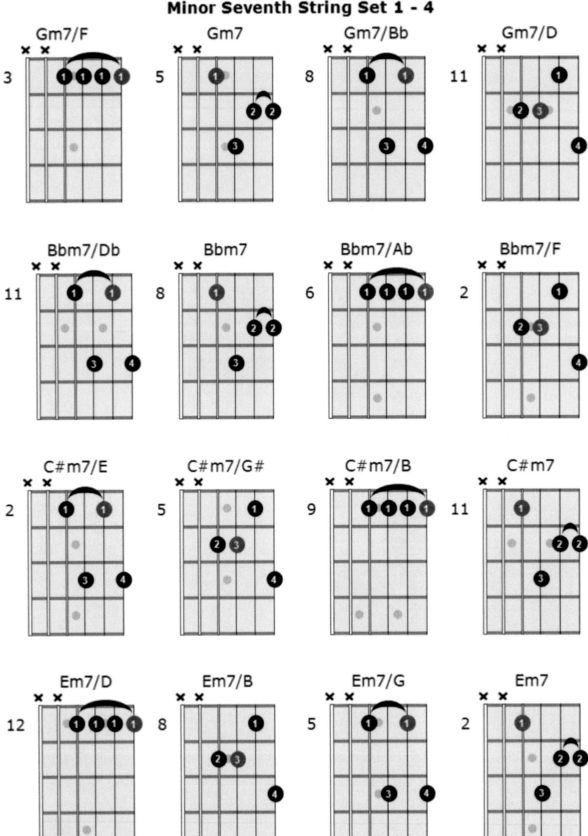

Minor Seventh String Set 2 - 5

Bm7
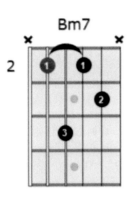

Bm7/D
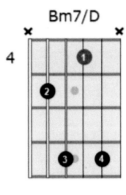

Bm7/F#
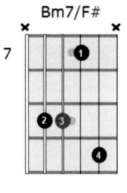

Bm7/A
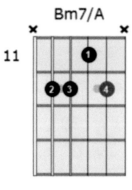

Dm7/A
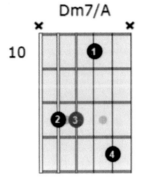

Dm7/F
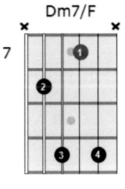

Dm7
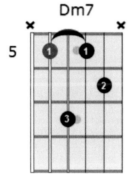

Dm7/C
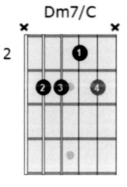

Fm7/C
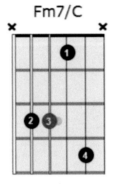

Fm7/Eb
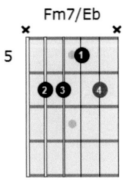

Fm7
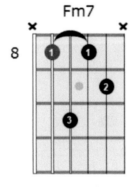

Fm7/Ab
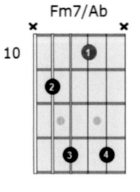

Abm7
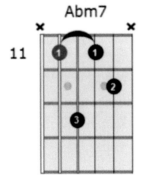

Abm7/Gb
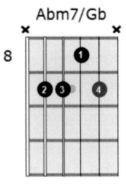

Abm7/Eb
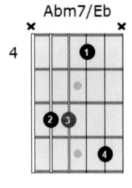

Abm7/B
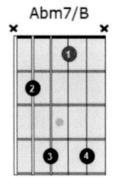

Minor Seventh String Sets 3 - 6

Ebm7/Gb
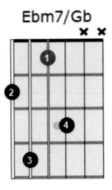

Ebm7/Bb
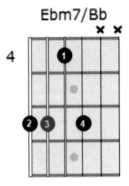

Ebm7/Db
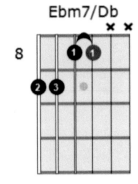

Ebm7
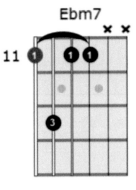

F#m7/E
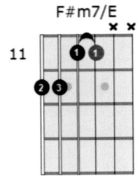

F#m7/C#
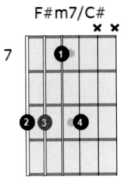

F#m7/A
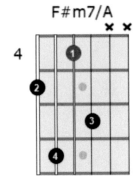

F#m7
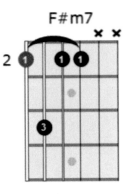

Am7/G
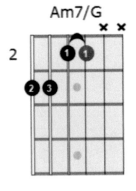

Am7
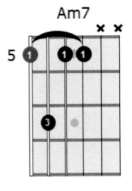

Am7/C
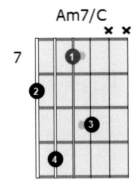

Am7/E
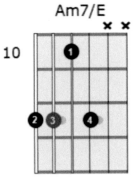

Cm7/Eb
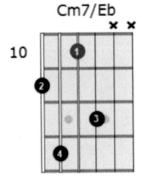

Cm7
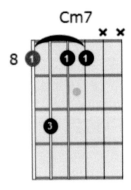

Cm7/Bb
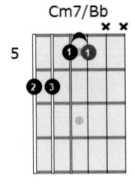

Cm7/G
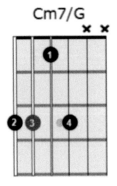

Lesson 3

Dominant Seventh Chords Over All Three String Sets

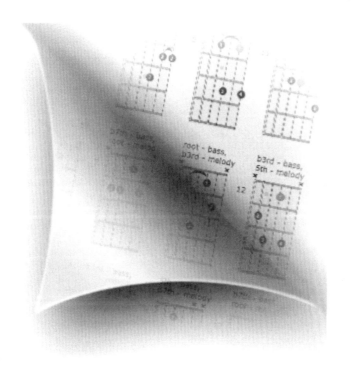

NOTES ABOUT LESSON 3

As in the last lesson, once you can finger and move between the chords, use the backing track to practice . Each chord gets four bars each and follows the order as found on the pages that follow.

Use backing track 2 for Lesson 3.

Dominant Seventh String Sets 1 - 4

B7/F#
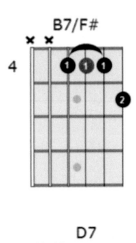

B7/A
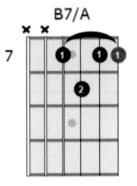

B7
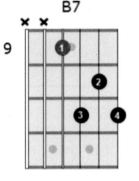

B7/D#
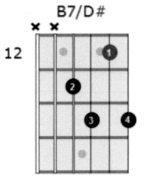

D7
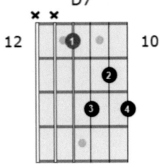

D7/C
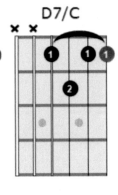

D7/A
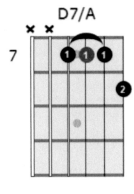

D7/F#
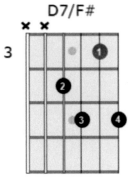

F7/Eb

F7
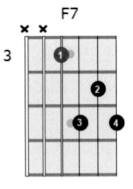

F7/A
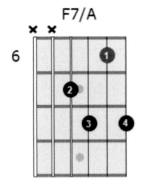

F7/C
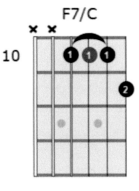

Ab7/C
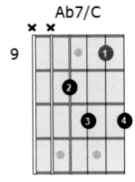

Ab7
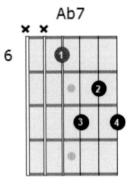

Ab7/Gb
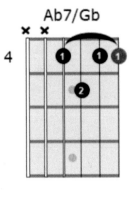

Ab7/Eb
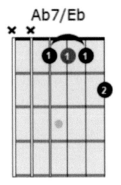

Dominant Seventh String Sets 2 - 5

Eb7/Db
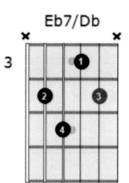

Eb7
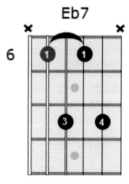

Eb7/G
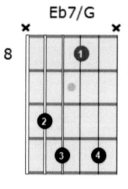

Eb7/Bb
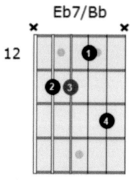

F#7/A#
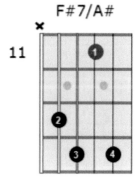

F#7
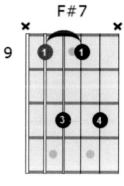

F#7/E
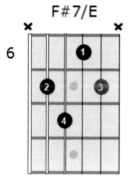

F#7/C#
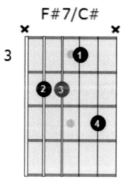

A7/C#
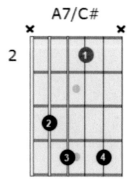

A7/E
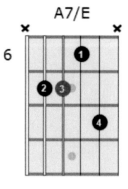

A7/G
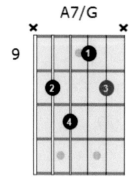

A7
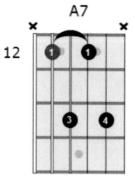

C7/Bb
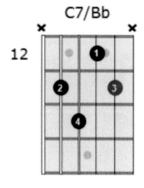

C7/G
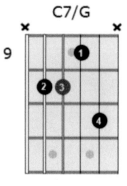

C7/E
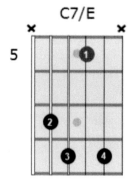

C7
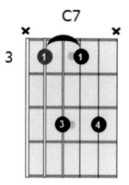

Dominant Sevenths String Sets 3 - 6

G7
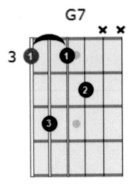

G7/B
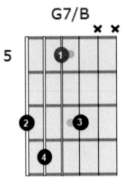

G7/D
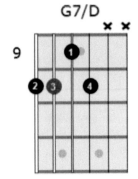

G7/F
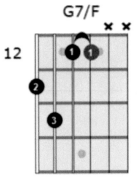

Bb7/F
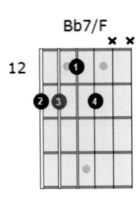

Bb7/D
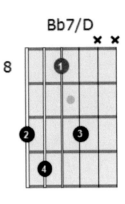

Bb7
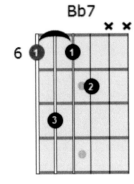

Bb7/Ab
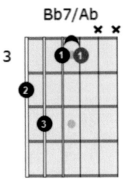

C#7/G#
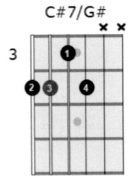

C#7/B
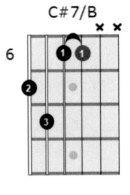

C#7
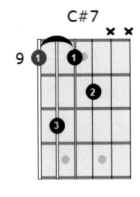

C#7/F
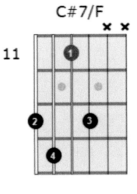

E7
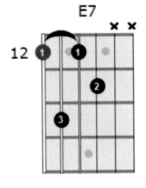

E7/D
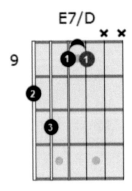

E7/B
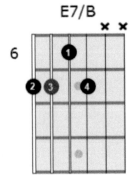

E7/G#
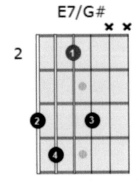

20

Lesson 4
Major Seventh Chords Over All Three String Sets

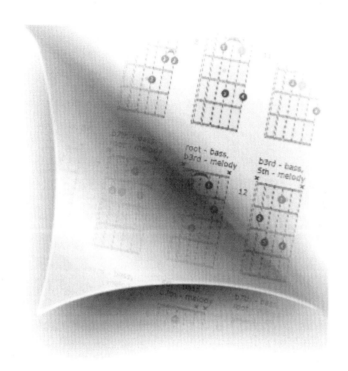

NOTES ABOUT LESSON 4

In this final lesson of section one, again, use the backing track to practice these chords. Follow the order as found on the pages that follow.

Use backing track 3 for Lesson 4.

Major Seventh String Sets 1 - 4

EbMaj7
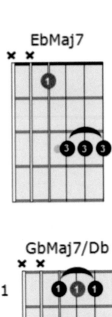

EbMaj7/G
4
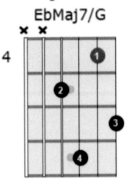

EbMaj7/Bb
8
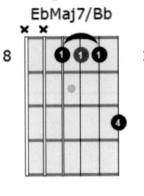

EbMaj7/D
11
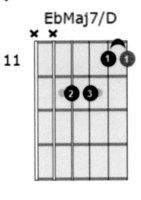

GbMaj7/Db
11
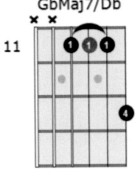

GbMaj7/Bb
7
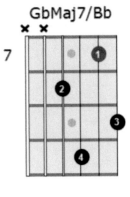

GbMaj7
4
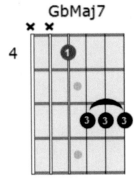

GbMaj7/F
2
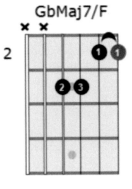

AMaj7/E
2
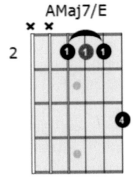

AMaj7/G#
5
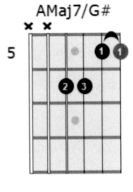

AMaj7
7
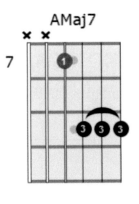

AMaj7/C#
10
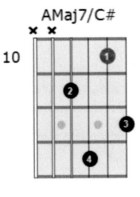

CMaj7
10
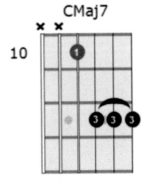

CMaj7/B
7
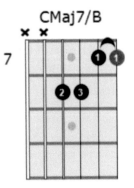

CMaj7/G
5
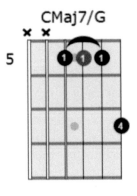

CMaj7/E
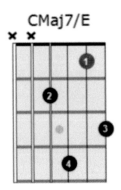

Major Seventh String Set 2 - 5

GMaj7/D
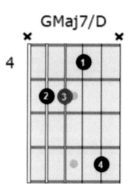

GMaj7/F#
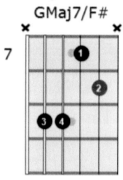

GMaj7
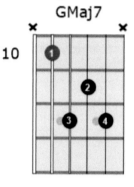

GMaj7/B
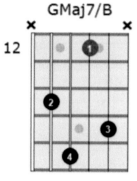

BbMaj7/A
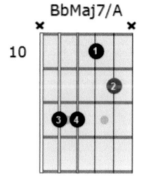

BbMaj7/F
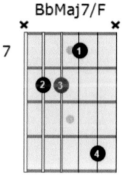

BbMaj7/D
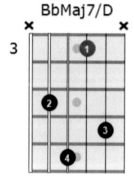

BbMaj7
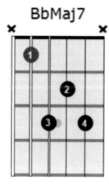

C#Maj7/C
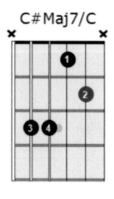

C#Maj7
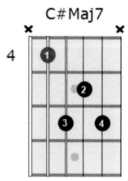

C#Maj7/F
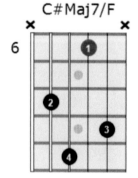

C#Maj7/G#
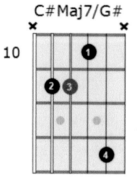

EMaj7/G#
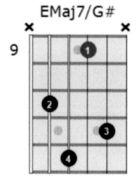

EMaj7
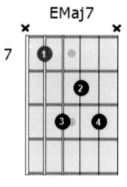

EMaj7/D#
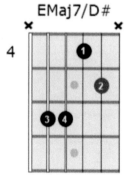

EMaj7/B
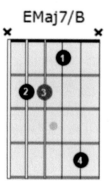

Major Seventh String Set 3 - 6

BMaj7/F#
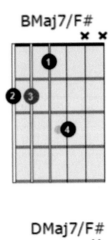

BMaj7/A#
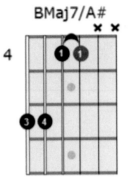

BMaj7
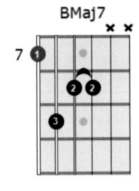

BMaj7/D#
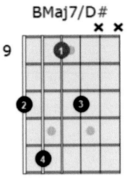

DMaj7/F#
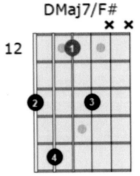

DMaj7
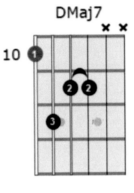

DMaj7/C#
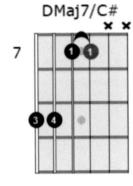

DMaj7/A
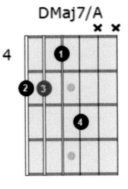

FMaj7
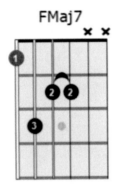

FMaj7/A
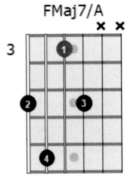

FMaj7/C
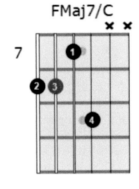

FMaj7/E
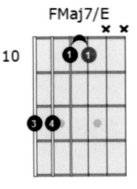

AbMaj7/Eb
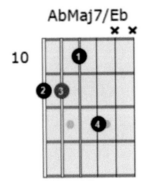

AbMaj7/C
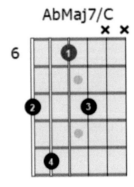

AbMaj7
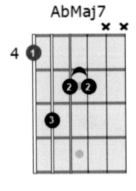

AbMaj7/G
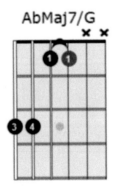

SECTION TWO

CHORD PROGRESSIONS

You should now have learned visually, physically and by name all the preceding chords in section one prior to beginning work on this section.

You will now use these three main chord types to create many well known progressions found in much of today's most popular music. The progressions which follow have been created to help you in three main areas:

1. To help your really know your chords by playing in progression.

2. The progressions have been created using strong voice leading between chords.

3. The keys used are deliberately distant from one another to help visualise chords in different keys.

Lesson 5
Major II - V - I Progressions

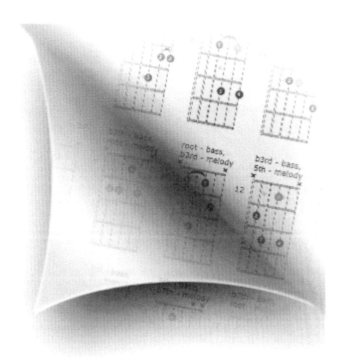

NOTES ABOUT LESSON 5

The II - V - I chord progression is one of the most widely used chord progressions in modern harmony. A large section of this book has been devoted to ensuring you have many examples to practice and learn across all string sets.

One word about the natural seventh in the bass re major seventh chords; use with extreme care. If you have a bass player then it will most often be fine to play the seventh in the bass. If you do not have a bass player take care, especially on the lower string sets as these sounds can sound very harsh.

Use backing tracks 4a (pages 28 - 33), 4b (pages 34 - 39) and 4c (pages 39 - 44) for this lesson. On the pages that follow, each chord line gets four beats each and the third chord is played for eight beats.

YOUTUBE VIDEO

View the video II V I Progression & Voice Leading at www.youtube.com/watch?v=TwgYu4pims8

II - V - I Progression up the neck in F Major string set 1 - 4

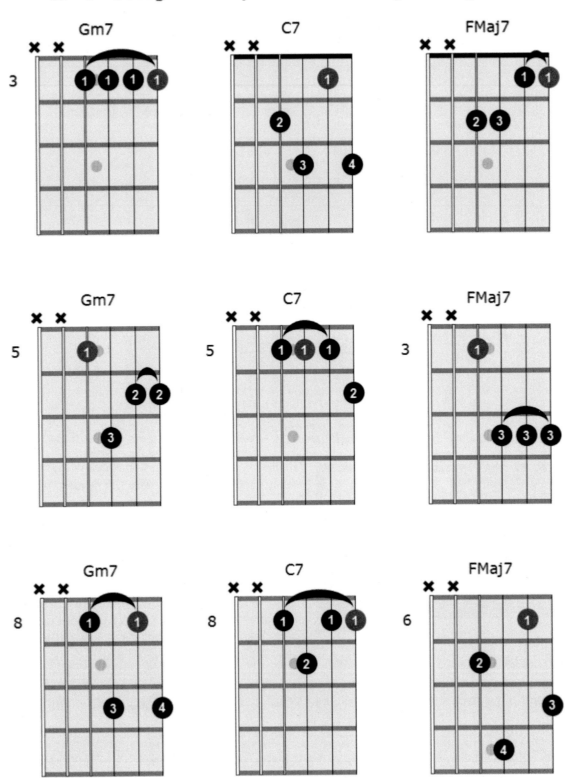

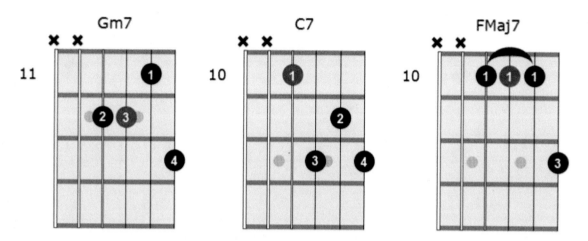

II - V - I Progression down the neck in Ab Major string set 1 - 4

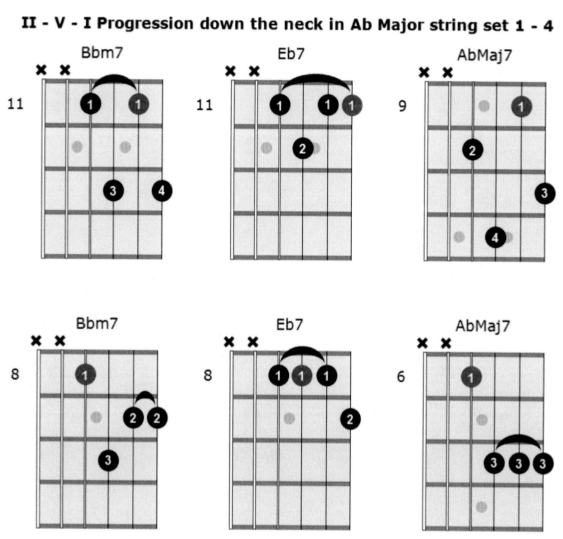

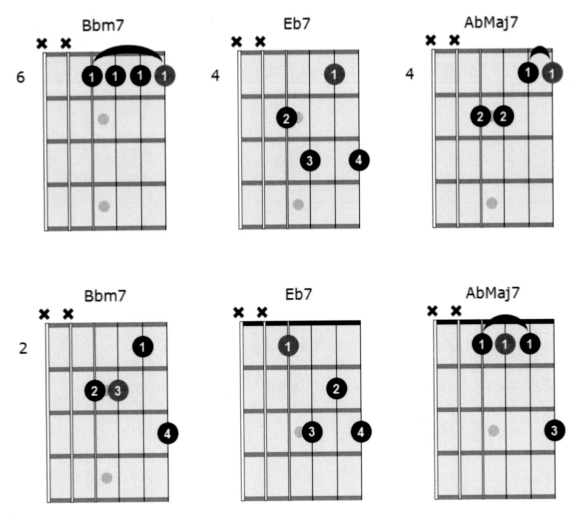

II - V - I Progression up the neck in B Major string set 1 - 4

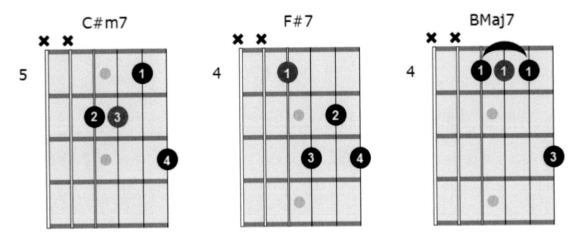

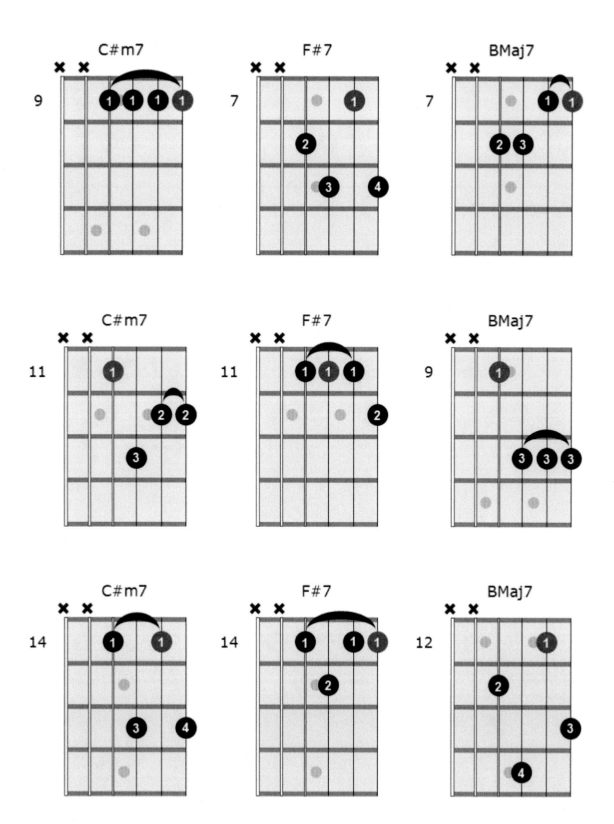

31

II - V - I Progression down the neck in D Major string set 1 - 4

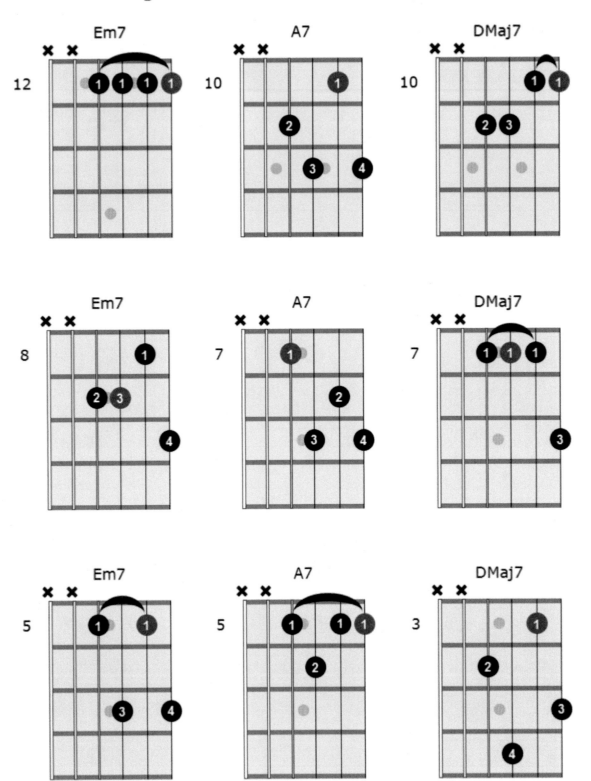

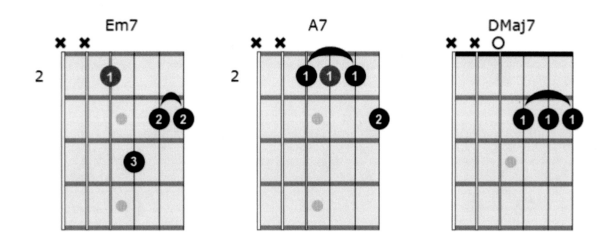

II - V - I Progression up the neck in A Major String Set 2 - 5

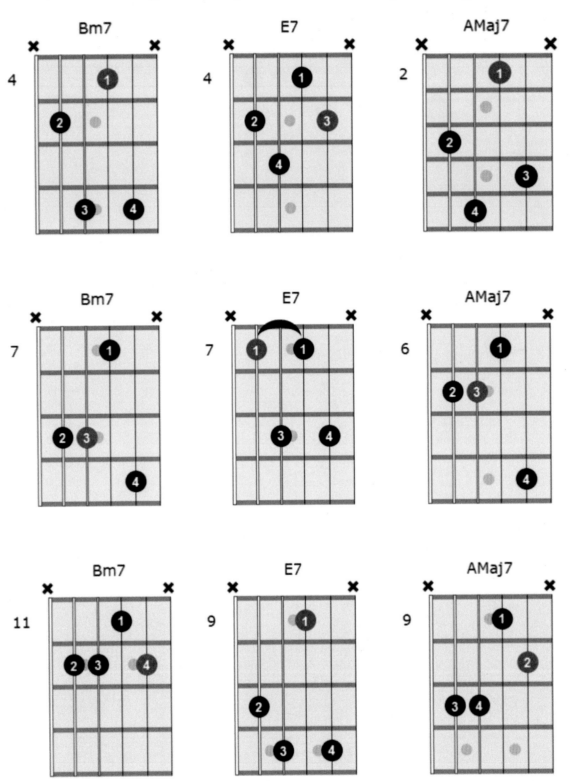

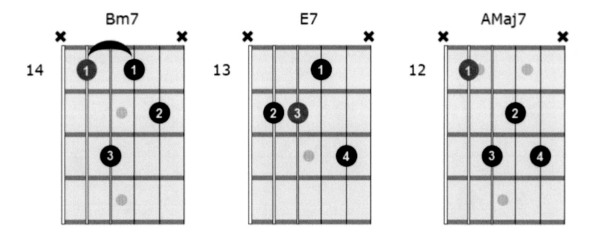

II - V - I Progression down the neck in C Major String Set 2 - 5

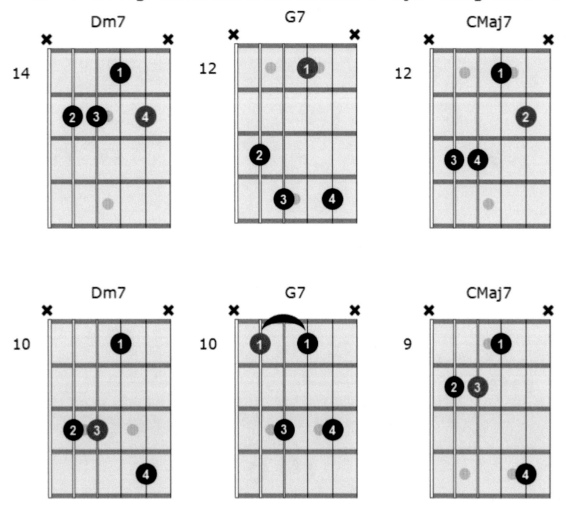

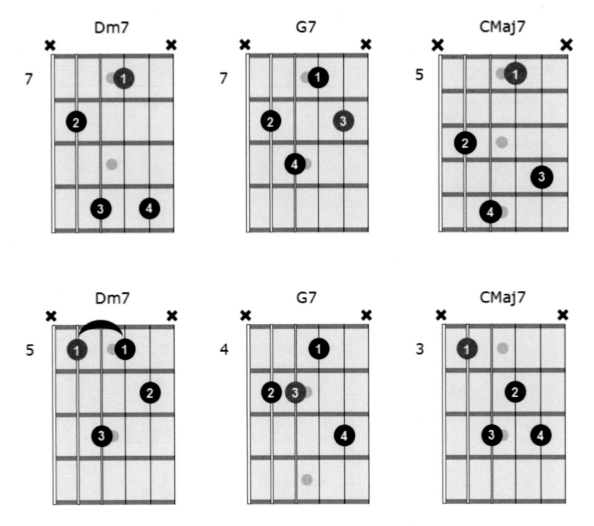

II - V - I Progression up the neck in Eb Major String Set 2 - 5

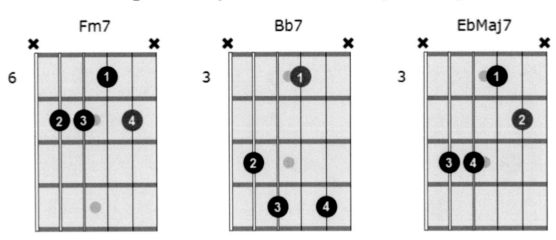

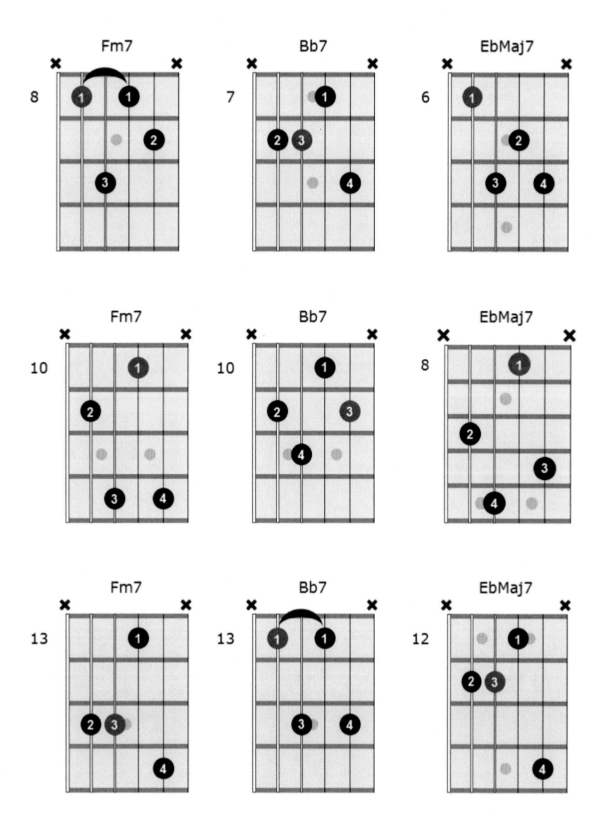

II - V - I down the neck in Gb Major String Set 2 -5

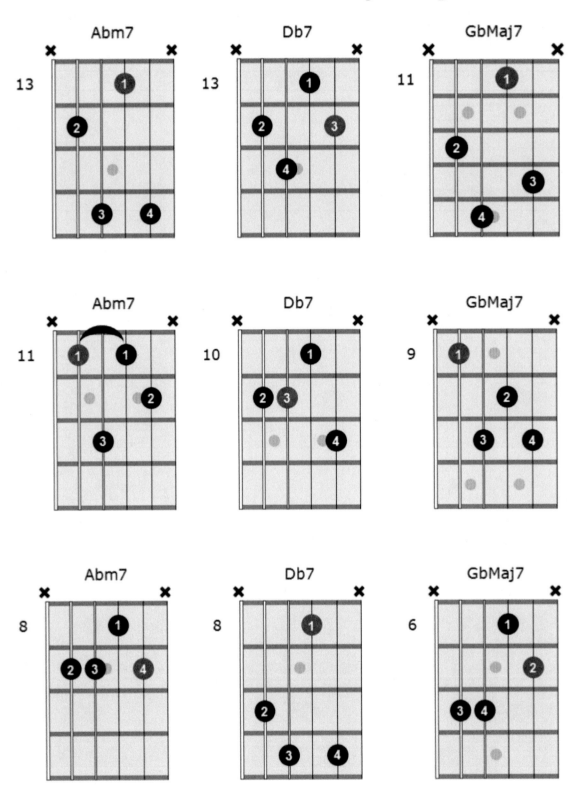

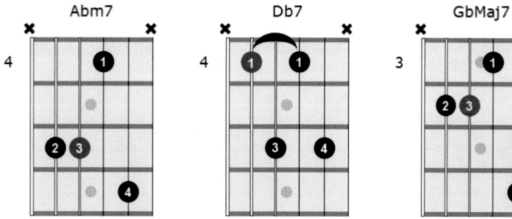

II - V - I up the neck in Db Major String Set 3 - 6

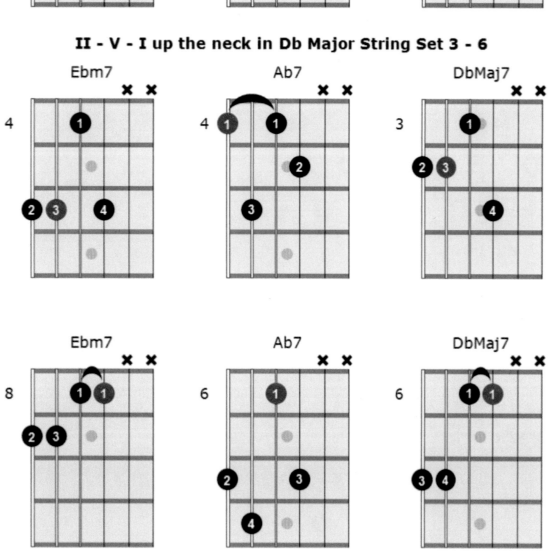

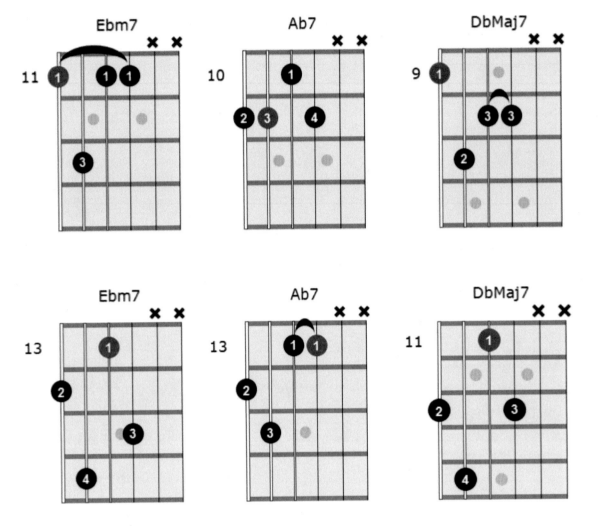

II - V - I down the neck in E Major String Set 3 - 6

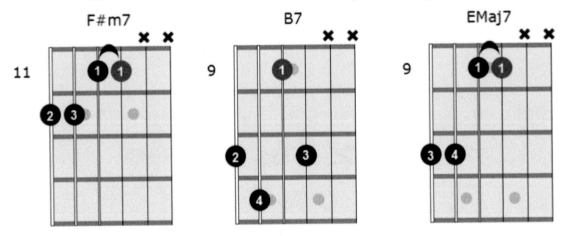

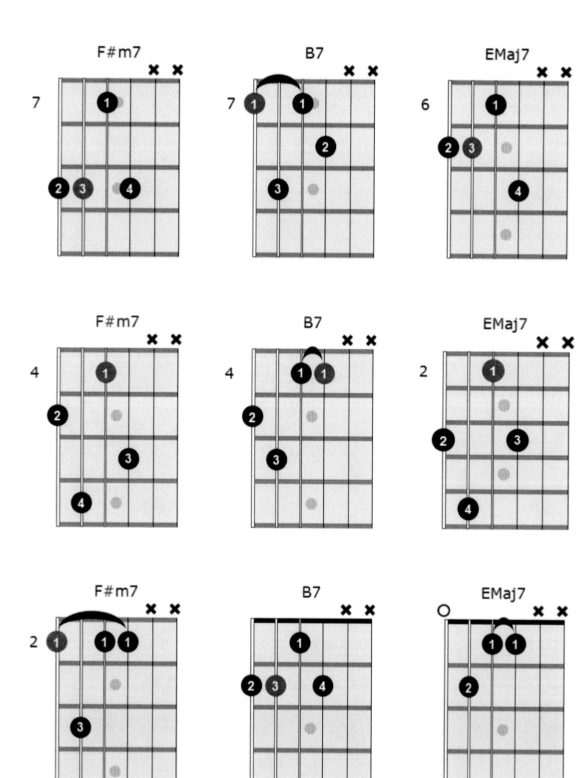

II - V - I up the neck in G Major String Set 3 - 6

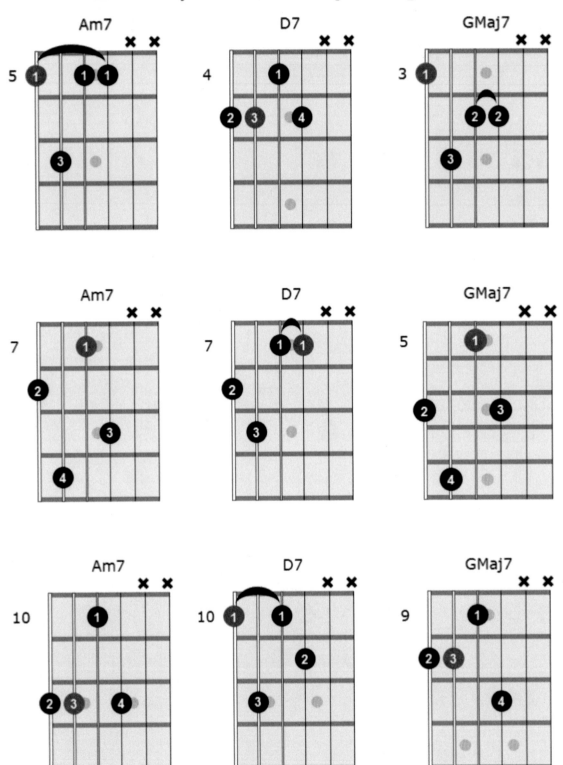

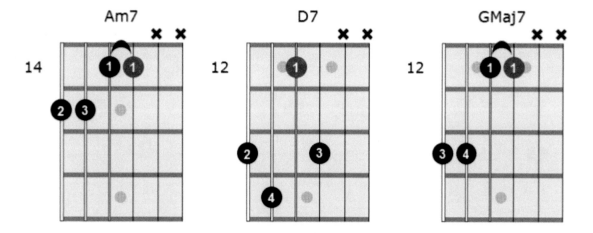

II - V - I down the neck in Bb Major String Set 3 - 6

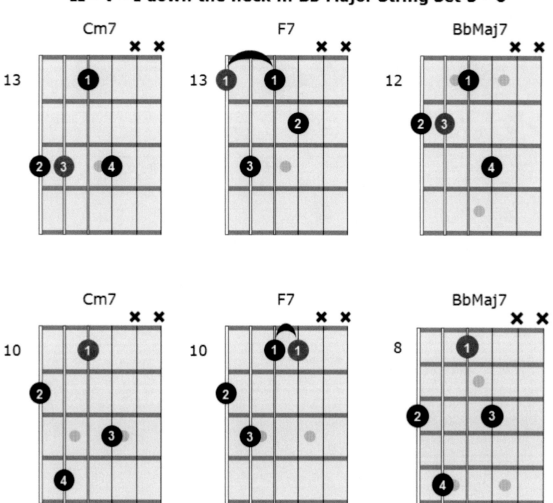

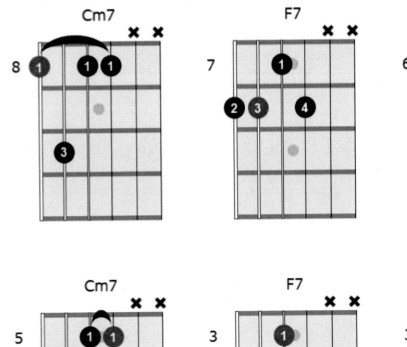

Lesson 6

From Dominant Seventh To Dominant Ninth

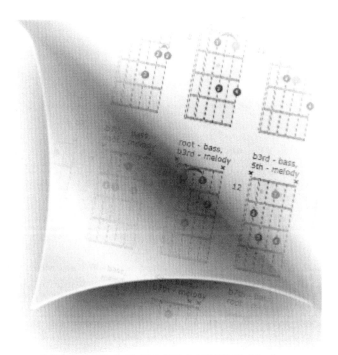

NOTES ABOUT LESSON 6

Drop Two Voicings Uncovered Lesson 4 - Dominant Seventh To Dominant Ninth

YOUTUBE VIDEO

Tonal colour can be added to dominant seventh chords by adding the 9th tone of the mixolydian scale. The 9th is the same tone as the 2nd, to find it simply play the note that is one tone (two frets) higher than the root note. This note is then added to the chord.

Remember, just because you can, does not mean you have to all the time! Don't just add ninths on everything. Used tastefully and within the context of the musical genre you are playing they are a very effective sound.

View video "Changing Dominant Seventh To Dominant Ninth" that accompanies Lesson 6 on Youtube at the following URL: www.youtube.com/watch?v=Rz1xgXZ2H3o

b7 to Dominant 9th String Set 1 - 4

C7   C9   C7   C9

C7   C9   C7   C9

b7 to Dominant 9th String Set 2 - 5

B7   B9   B7   B9

B7   B9   B7   B9

46

b7 to Dominant 9th String Set 3 - 6

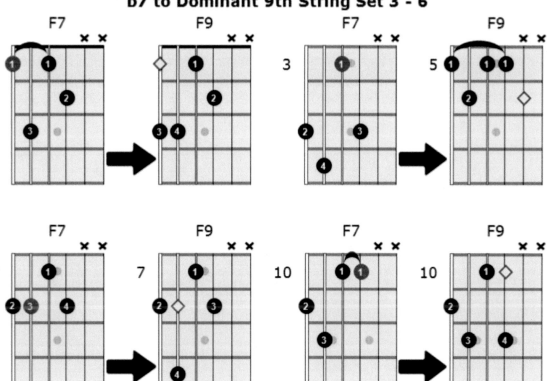

Lesson 7

Extending The Major II - V - I Progression Using Synonyms

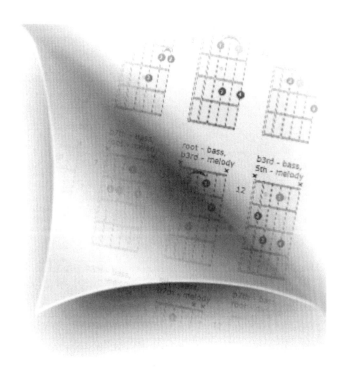

NOTES ABOUT LESSON 7

One of the best ways to expand your chordal ideas is to understand and utilise chordal synonyms. This ideas is also used in a later lesson, however, in this lesson you are eased into the use of synonyms with an easy to understand and execute concept.

Use the following backing tracks to practice these chords 5a (pages 50 - 53), 5b (pages 54 - 57), 5c (pages 58 - 61). Each chord gets four beats each and follows the order as found on the pages that follow.

YOUTUBE VIDEO

View the video "Chord Synonyms & Adding The Major Sixth Chord" that accompanies Lesson 7 on Youtube at the following URL: www.youtube.com/watch?v=Rz1xgXZ2H30

II - V9 - IMaj7 - 6 up the neck in G Major String Set 1 - 4

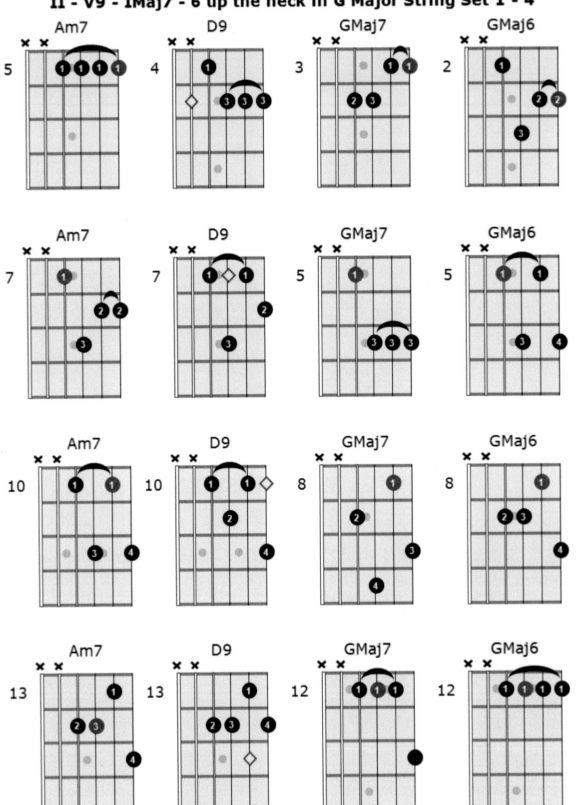

II - V9 - IMaj7 - 6 down the neck in Bb Major String Set 1 - 4

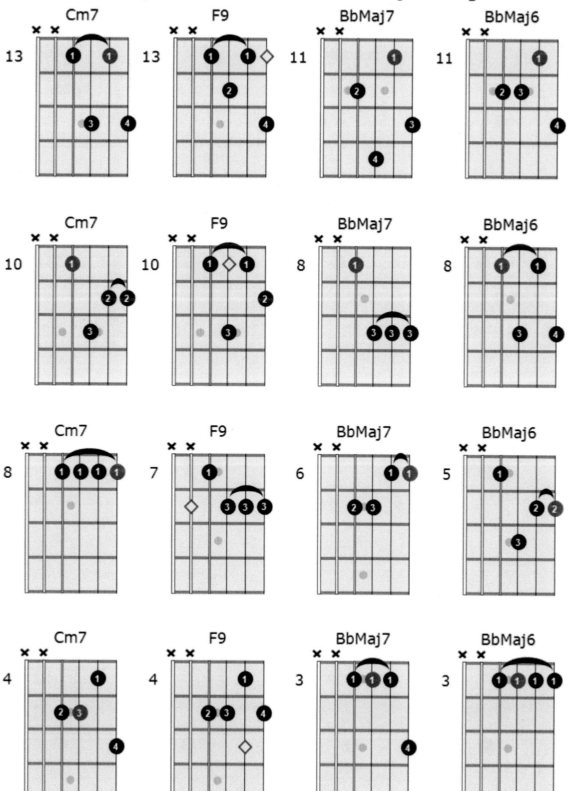

II - V9 - IMaj7 - 6 up the neck in C# Major String Set 1 - 4

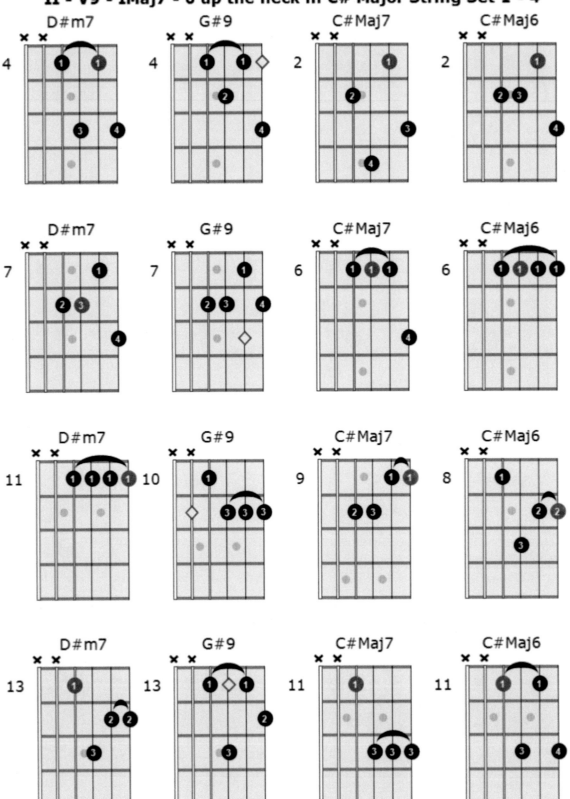

II - V9 - IMaj7 - 6 down the neck in E Major String Set 1 - 4

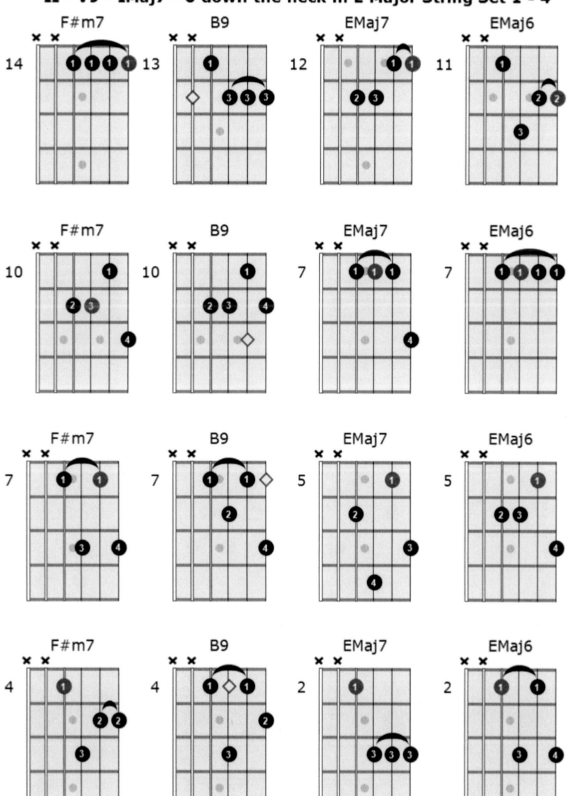

II - V9 - IMaj7 - 6 up the neck in F Major String Set 2 - 5

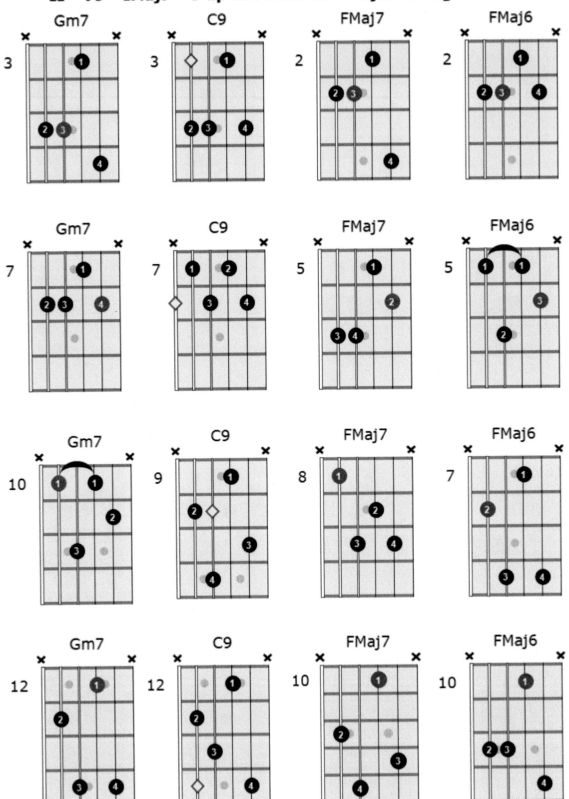

II - V9 - IMaj7 - 6 down the neck in Ab Major String Set 2 - 5

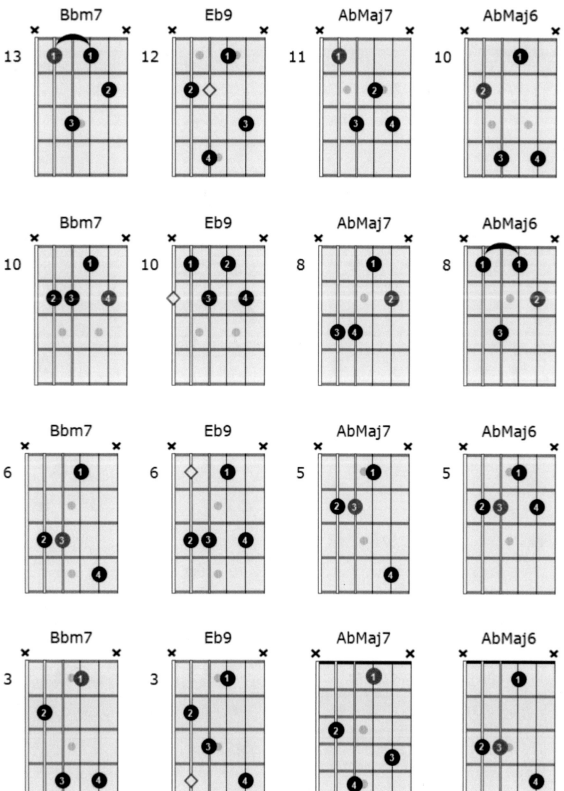

II - V9 - IMaj7 - 6 up the neck in B Major String Set 2 - 5

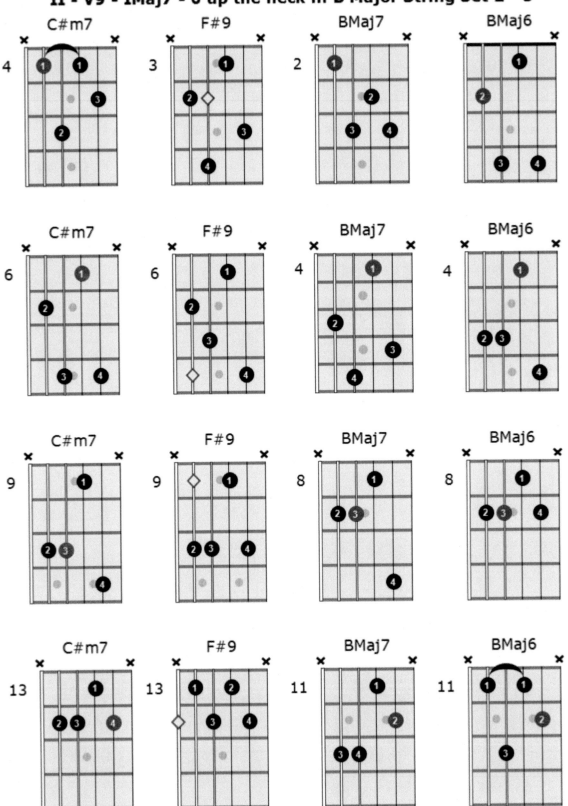

II - V9 - IMaj7 - 6 down the neck in D Major String Set 2 - 5

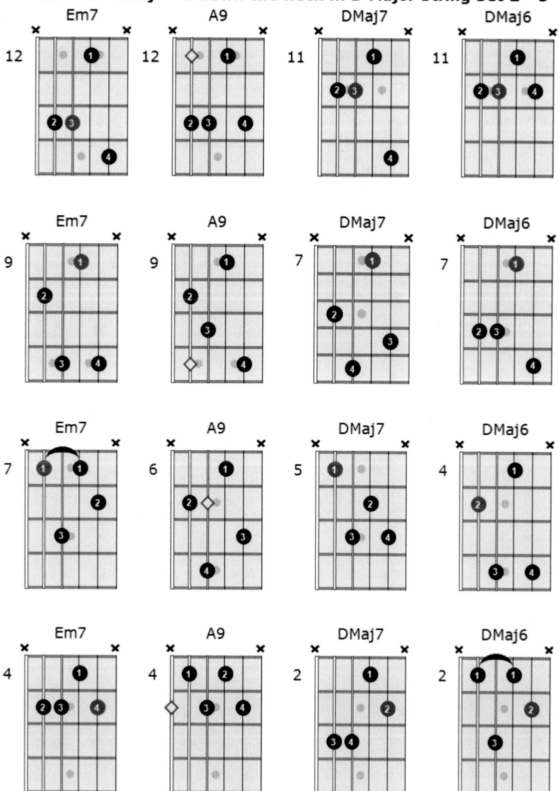

II - V9 - IMaj7 - 6 up the neck in C Major String Set 3 - 6

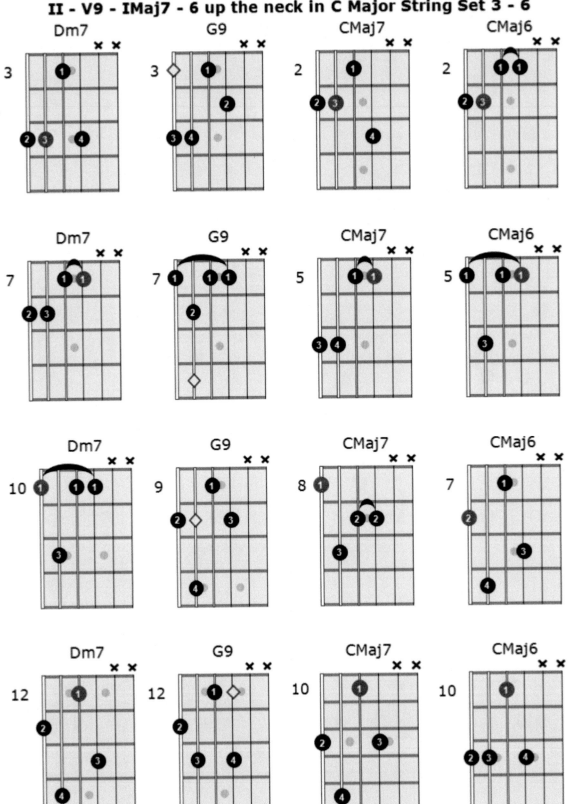

II - V9 - IMaj7 - 6 down the neck in Eb Major String Set 3 - 6

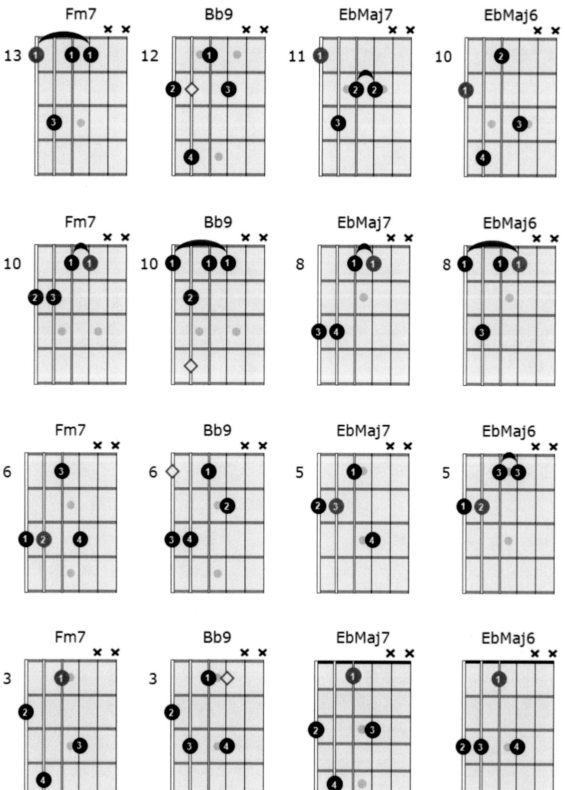

II - V9 - IMaj7 - 6 up the neck in Gb Major String Set 3 - 6

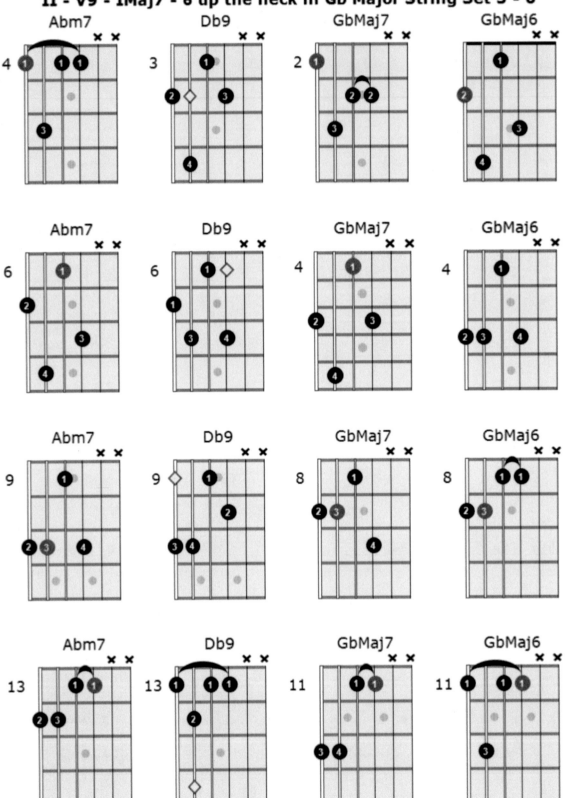

II - V9 - IMaj7 - 6 down the neck in A Major String Set 3 - 6

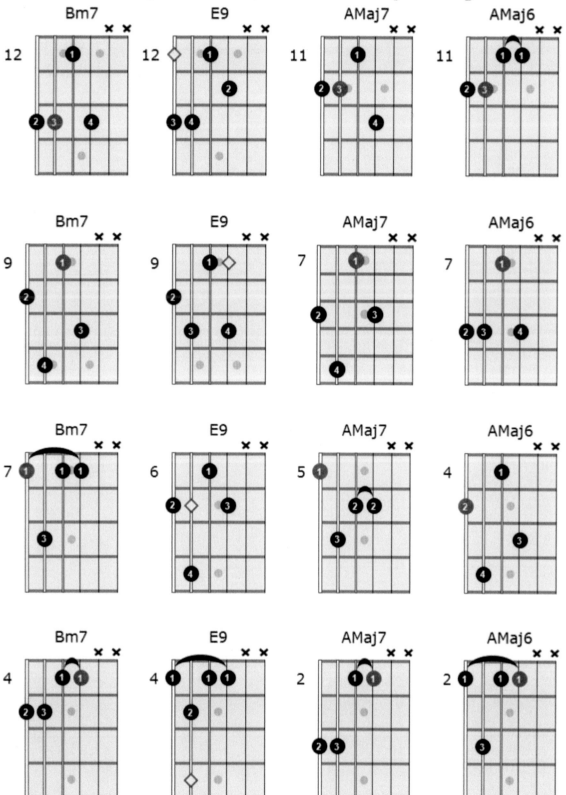

Lesson 8

The Major I - VI - II - V Progression

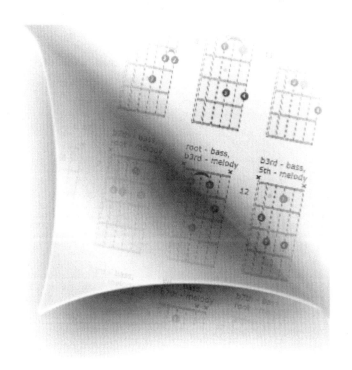

NOTES ABOUT LESSON 8

This lesson is all about reinforcing the knowledge that you have gained so far. The video will do most of the heavy lifting as far as explaining the finer details, however, the main idea is to have you playing the same chord progression up the neck in different positions.

Use the following backing tracks to practice these chords 6a (pages 64 - 66), 6b (page 67), 6c (page 68). Each chord gets four beats each and follows the order as found on the pages that follow.

YOUTUBE VIDEO

View the video "Playing Up The Neck & Through A Chord Progression" that accompanies Lesson 8 on Youtube at the following URL: www.youtube.com/watch?v=iJHM54EHs3M

I - VI - II - V up the neck in A Major string set 1 - 4

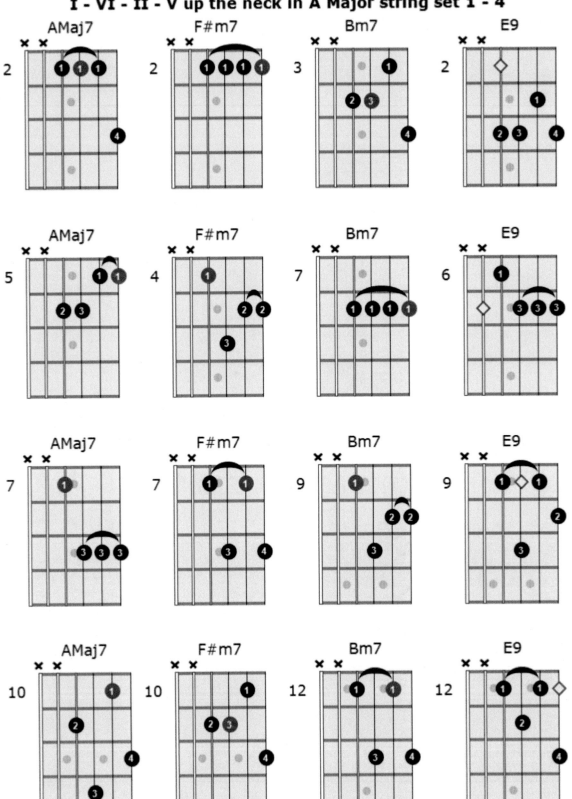

I - VI - II - V up the neck in Bb Major string set 2 - 5

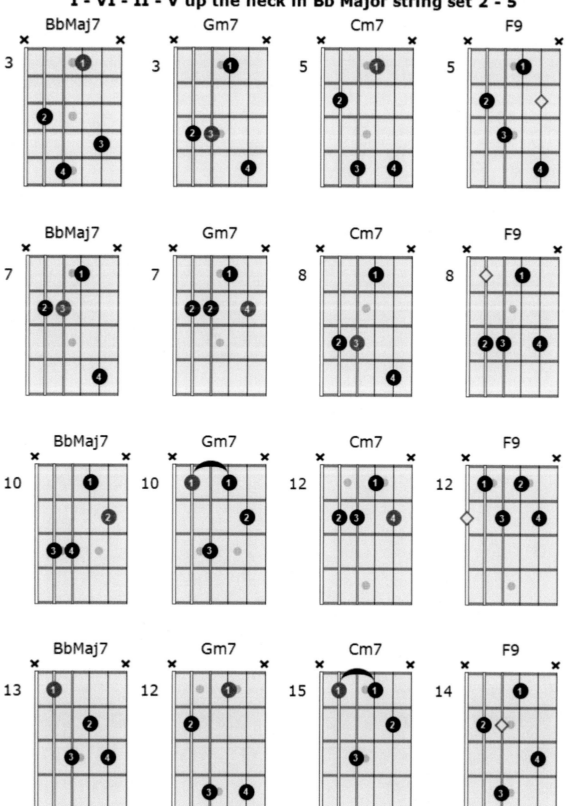

I - VI - II - V up the neck in Eb Major string set 3 - 6

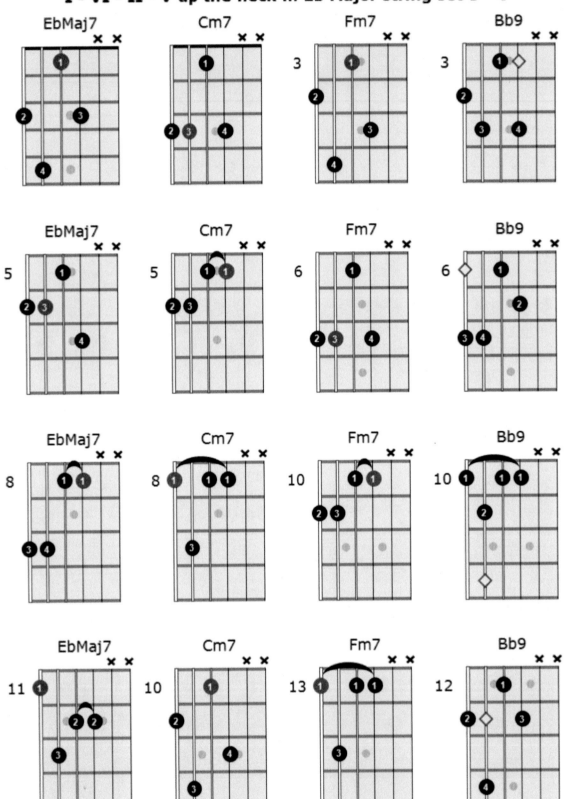

I - VI - II - V across the neck in G Major

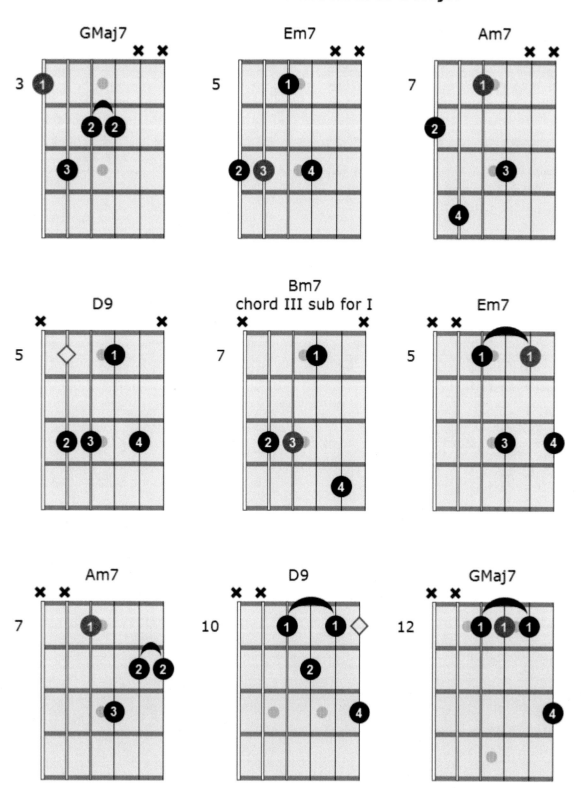

I - VI - II - V across the neck in D Major

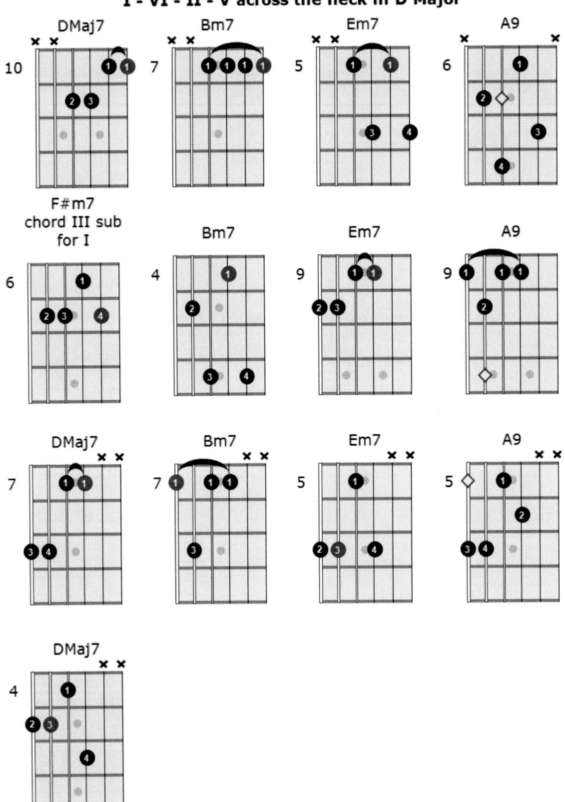

Lesson 9

Chords Played Diatonically Through Major Keys

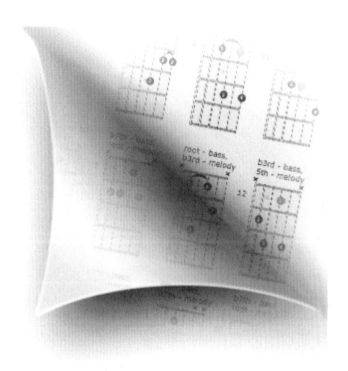

NOTES ABOUT LESSON 9

Understanding how music keys work is incredibly important and that is why a large lesson has been devoted to it in this text. There is no backing track for this lesson, rather you should go through all twelve examples and ensure that you understand all the points covered in depth from the lesson video.

Once you understand how keys work you will open up a whole new level of opportunities with regards you chordal playing and how you use chords.

YOUTUBE VIDEO

View the video "Understanding Major Diatonic Chord" that accompanies Lesson 9 on Youtube at the following URL: www.youtube.com/watch?v=iJHM54EHs3M

Four Note Diatonic System In F Major String Set 1 - 4

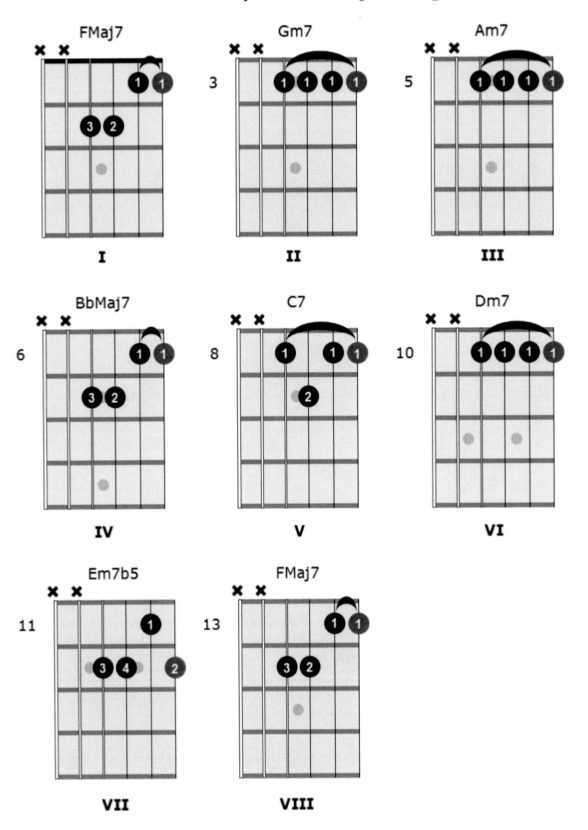

Four Note Diatonic System In Eb Major String Set 1 - 4

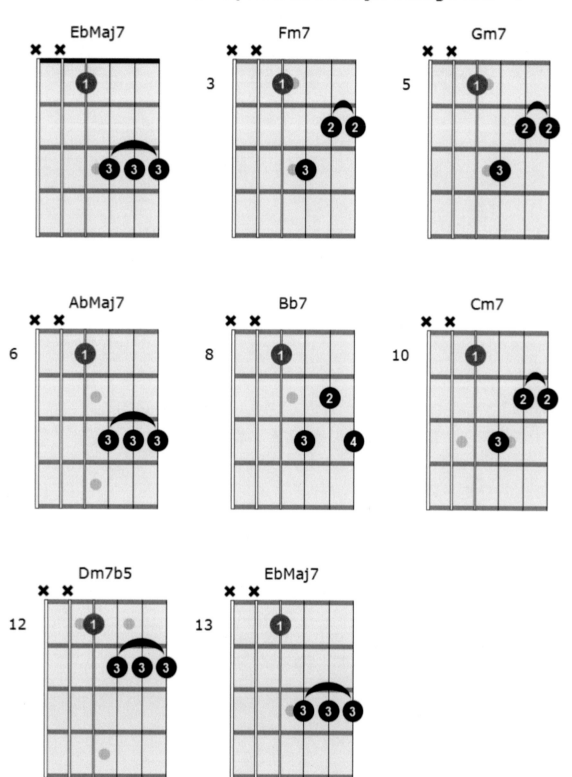

Four Note Diatonic System In C Major String Set 1 - 4

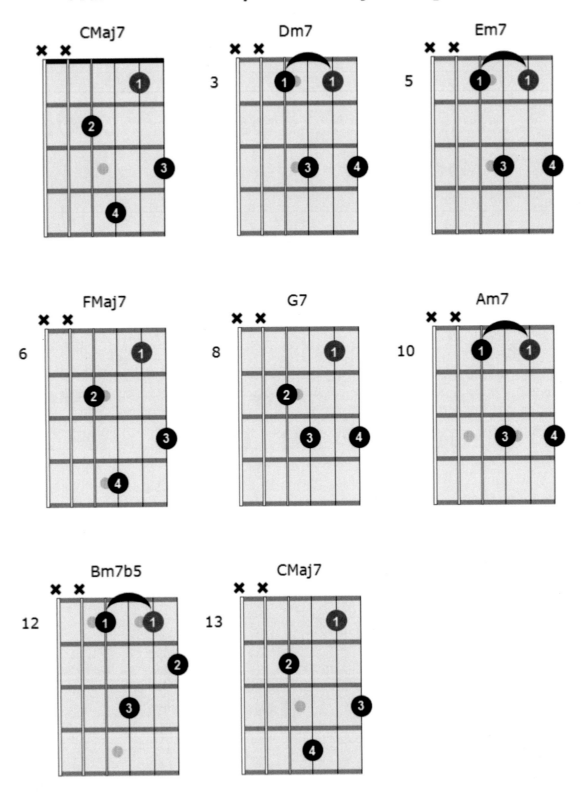

CMaj7

Dm7

Em7

FMaj7

G7

Am7

Bm7b5

CMaj7

Four Note Diatonic System In Ab Major String Set 1 - 4

AbMaj7
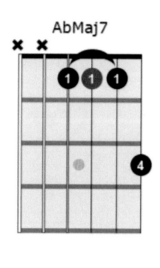

Bbm7
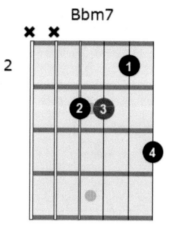

Cm7
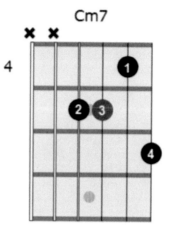

DbMaj7
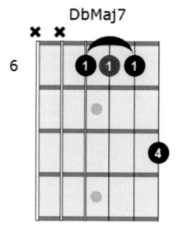

Eb7
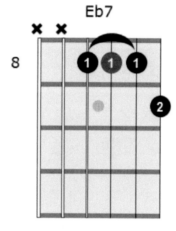

Fm7
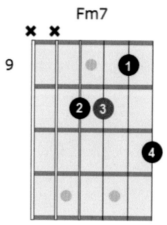

Gm7b5
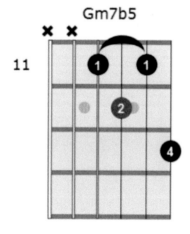

AbMaj7
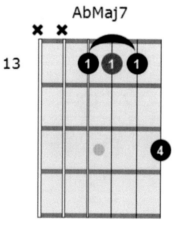

Four Note Diatonic System In Bb Major String Set 2 - 5

BbMaj7
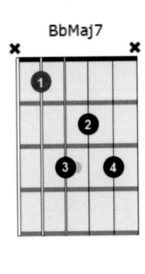

Cm7
3
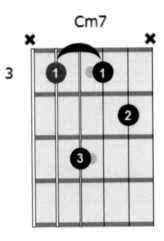

Dm7
5
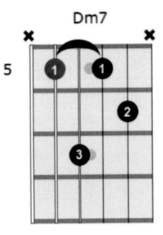

EbMaj7
6
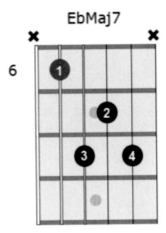

F7
8
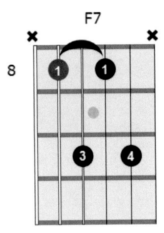

Gm7
10
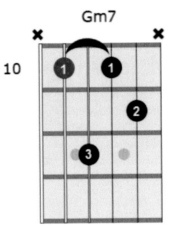

Am7b5
12
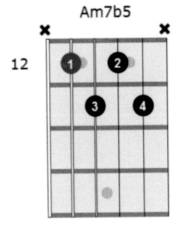

BbMaj7
13
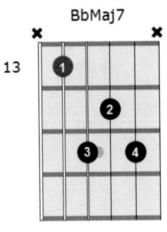

Four Note Diatonic System In Bb Major String Set 2 - 5

AbMaj7

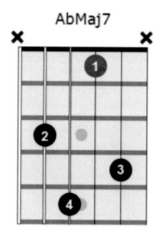

Bbm7

3

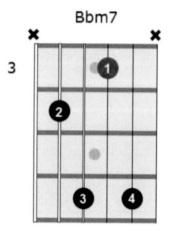

Cm7

5

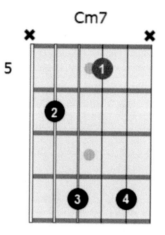

DbMaj7

6

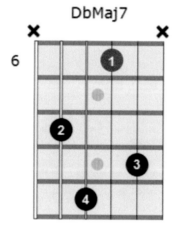

Eb7

8

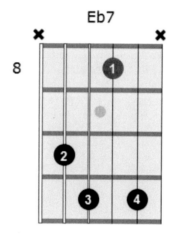

Fm7

10

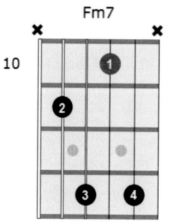

Gm7b5

12

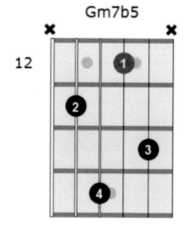

AbMaj7

13

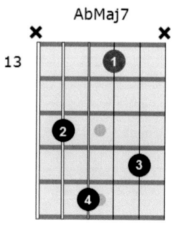

Four Note Diatonic System In E Major String Set 2 - 5

EMaj7
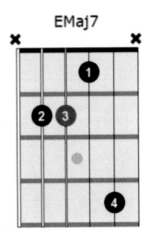

F#m7
2
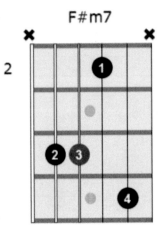

G#m7
4
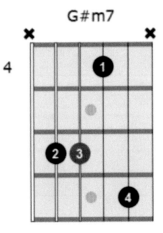

AMaj7
6
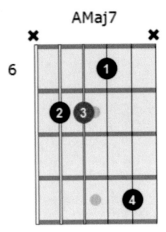

B7
8
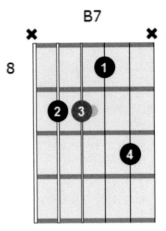

C#m7
9
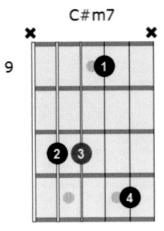

D#m7b5
11
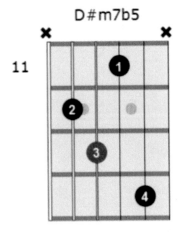

AMaj7
13
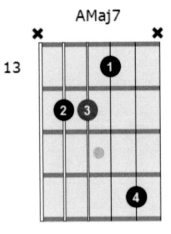

Four Note Diatonic System In Db Major String Set 2 - 5

DbMaj7
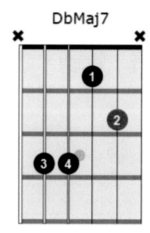

Ebm7
3
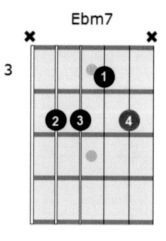

Fm7
5
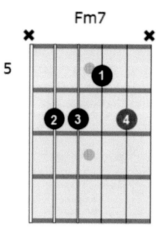

GbMaj7
6
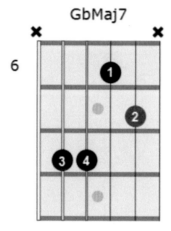

Ab7
8
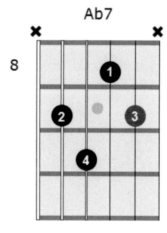

Bbm7
10
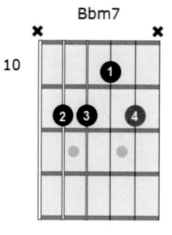

Cm7b5
11
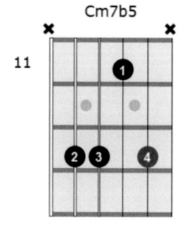

DbMaj7
13
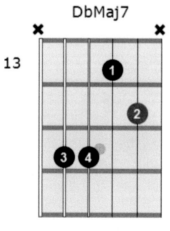

Four Note Diatonic System In F Major String Set 3 - 6

FMaj7
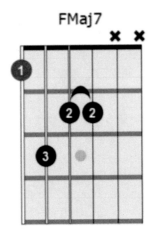

Gm7
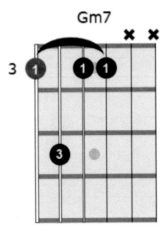

Am7
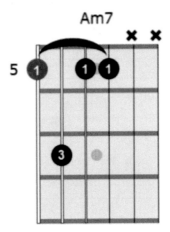

BbMaj7
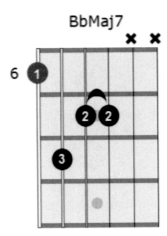

C7
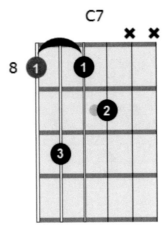

Dm7
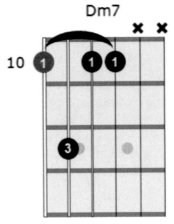

Em7b5
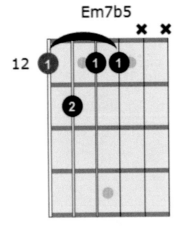

FMaj7
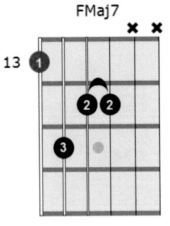

Four Note Diatonic System In F Major String Set 3 - 6

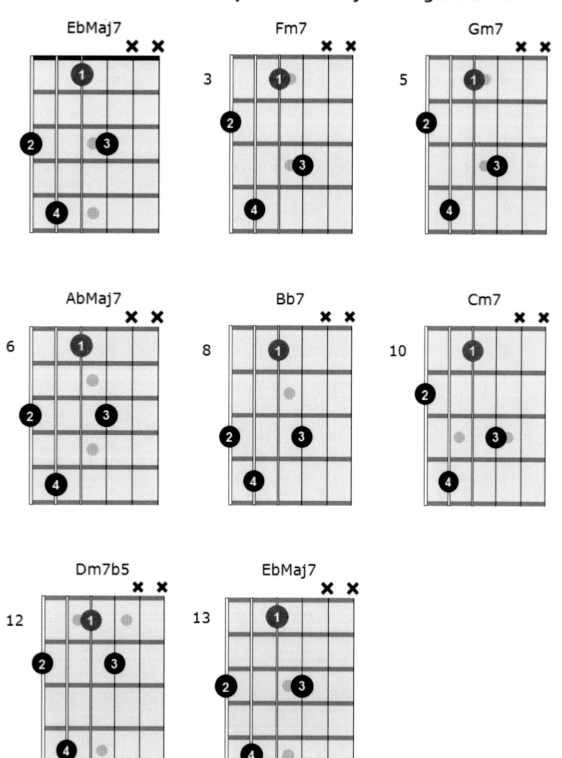

Four Note Diatonic System In B Major String Set 3 - 6

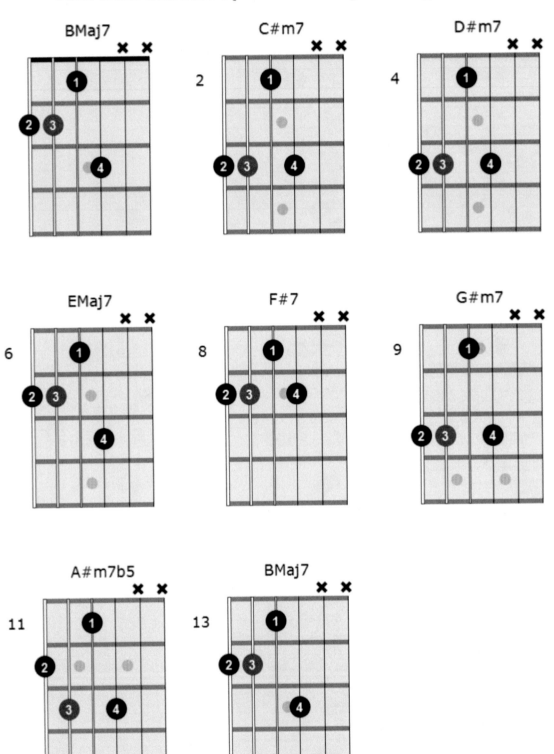

BMaj7

C#m7

D#m7

EMaj7

F#7

G#m7

A#m7b5

BMaj7

Four Note Diatonic System In Ab Major String Set 3 - 6

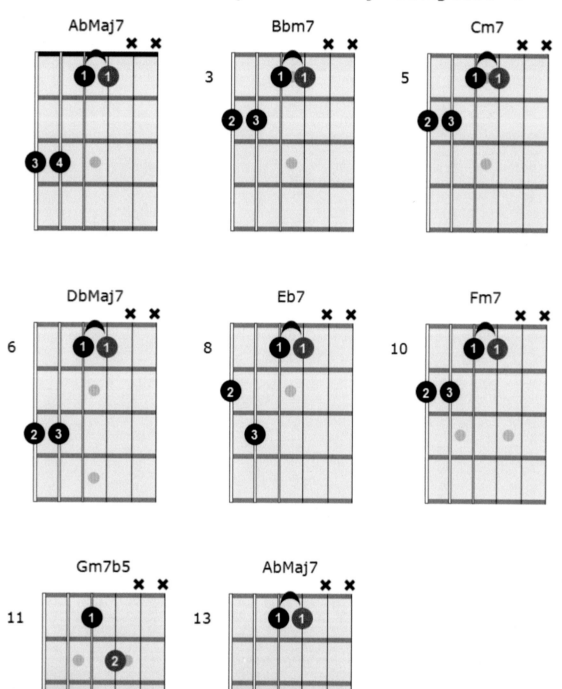

Lesson 10

The Major I - VI - IV - V Progression

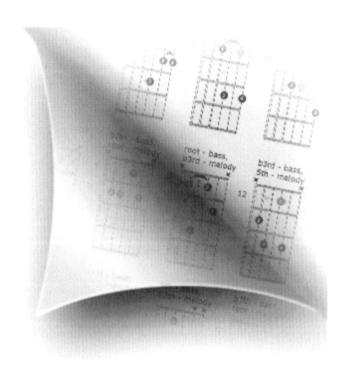

NOTES ABOUT LESSON 10

Drop Two Voicings Uncovered Lesson 8 - The I - VI - IV - V Progression & More!

This lesson seems fairly straight forward, however, you must see the video that accompanies the lesson. It is without doubt one of the more challenging videos but for those that persevere, understand and apply the nuggets of gold in it; they'll never look back. Basically, it shows you how to multiply many of the chord shapes you currently use by a factor of three. So ensure you watch it.

Use backing track number 7 in conjunction with the chords that follow. Each chord gets four beats each.

YOUTUBE VIDEO

View the video "The I - VI - IV - V Progression & More! " that accompanies Lesson 10 on Youtube at the following URL: www.youtube.com/watch?v=qQvgM2cPyMU

I - VI - IV - V down the neck in C Major String Set 1 - 4

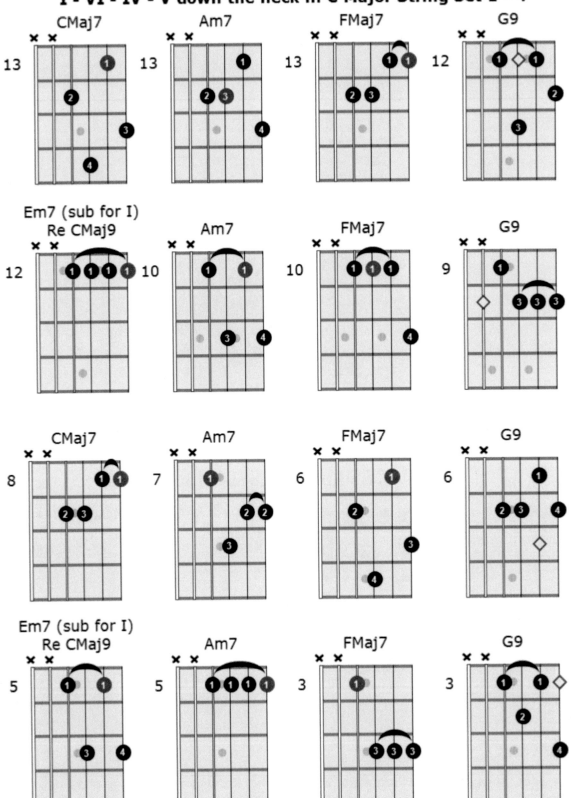

I - VI - IV - V up the neck in Ab Major String Set 2 - 5

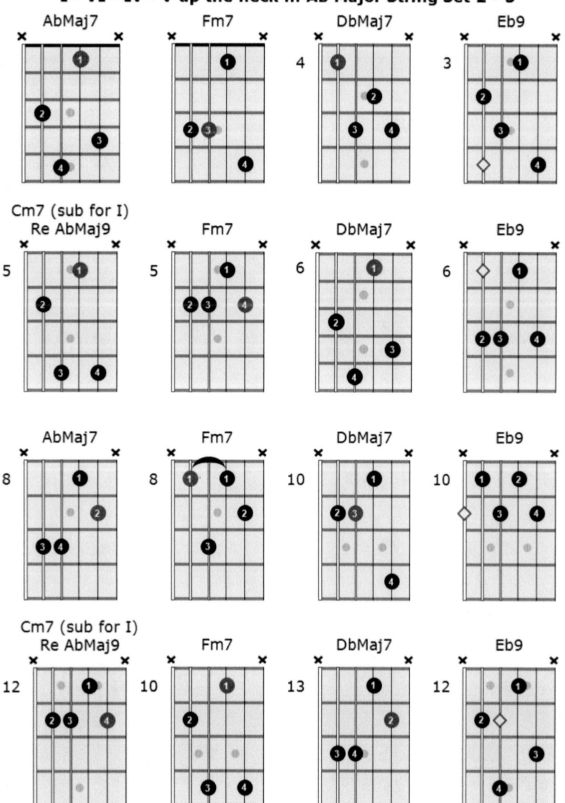

I - VI - IV - V up the neck in F Major String Set 3 - 6

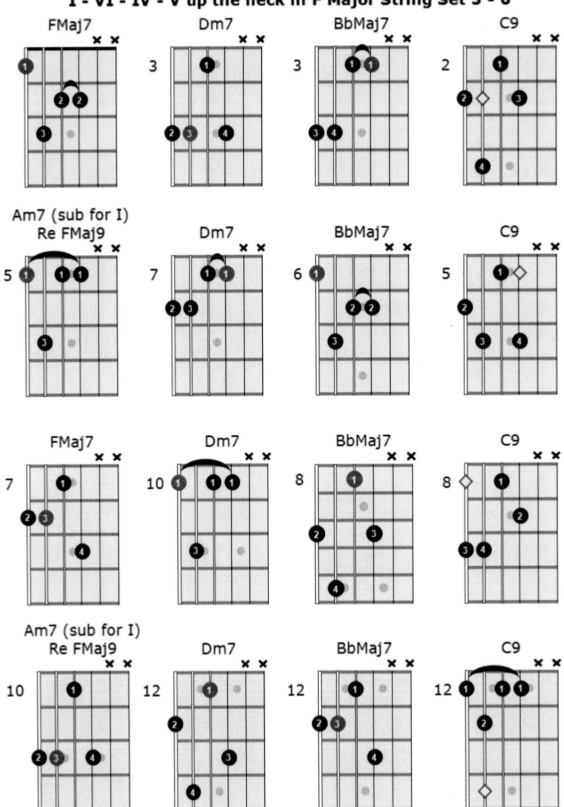

86

SECTION THREE

MINOR CHORDS & PROGRESSIONS

Lesson 11 - Minor II - V - I progressions

Lesson 12 - Minor I - VI - II - V progressions

Lesson 13 - Minor I - VI - II - V progressions across the fingerboard

You should now have learned visually, physically and by name all the preceding chords in section two prior to beginning work on this section. You should now also have memorised the progressions and the theoretical concepts given in the previous videos.

If you have accomplished the above then it is time for you to move on. We are now going to work within minor keys and the main things we need to cover are:

1. Understanding the the options that are available within minor keys re harmonisation.

2. Ensuring that the chords we use give good resolution to the tonic chord.

3. Working towards playing through chord progressions across the fingerboard.

Lesson 11
Minor II - V - I Progressions

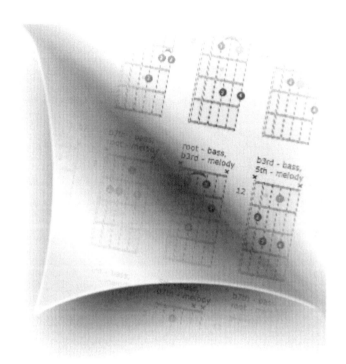

NOTES ABOUT LESSON 11

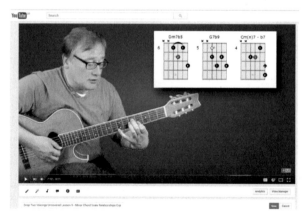

Choice can be seen as a good thing, however, sometimes it can just be confusing for people. This lesson shows you how to play II - V - I minor progressions but the video goes into depth around the choices that you have when faced with minor key centres. This is a great way of really getting to know why certain minor scales and keys are used more than others.

Use backing track number 8 in conjunction with the chords that follow. The first two chord on each line get four beats each, the last chord eight beats.

YOUTUBE VIDEO

View the video "Minor Chord Scale Relationships Explained" that accompanies Lesson 11 on Youtube at the following URL: www.youtube.com/watch?v=i3VboG-qcQs

II - V - I up the neck in C minor String Set 1 - 4

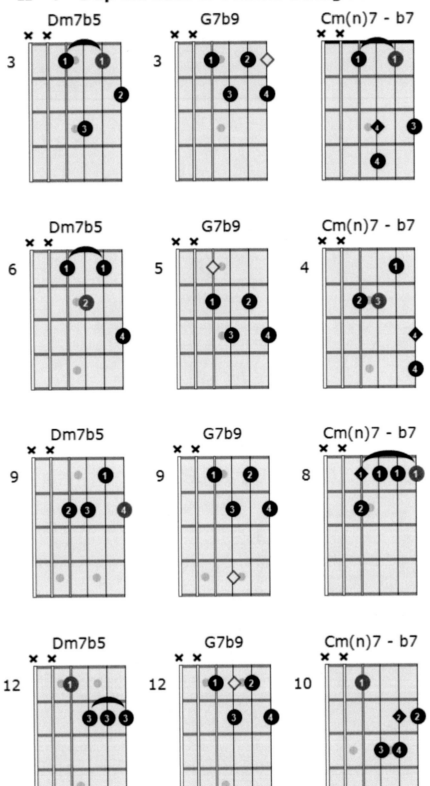

II - V - I up the neck in F minor String Set 2 - 5

Gm7b5
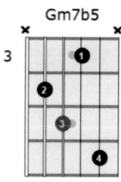

C7b9
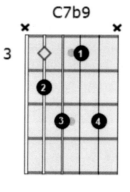

Fm(n)7 - b7
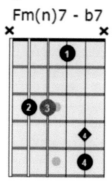

Gm7b5
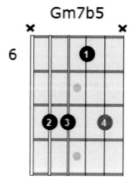

C7b9
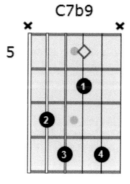

Fm(n)7 - b7
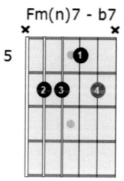

Gm7b5
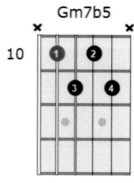

C7b9
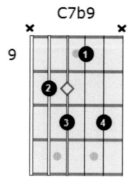

Fm(n)7 - b7
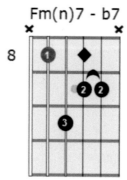

Gm7b5
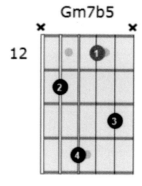

C7b9
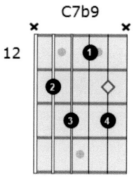

Fm(n)7 - b7
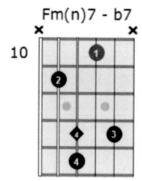

II - V - I up the neck in Ab minor String Set 3 - 6

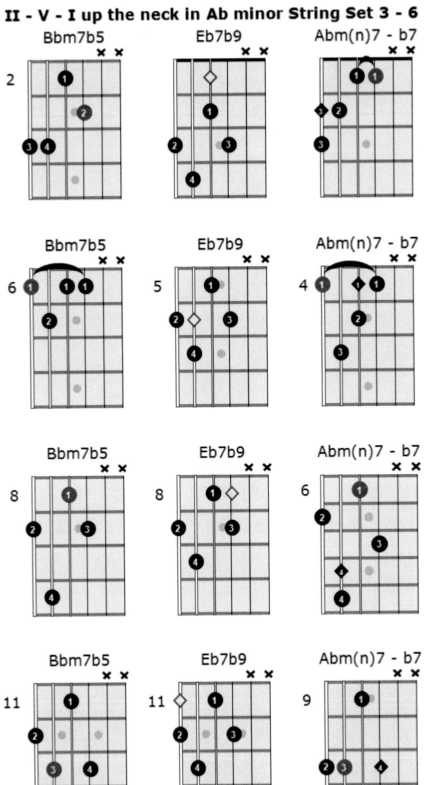

Lesson 12

Minor I - VI - II - V Progressions

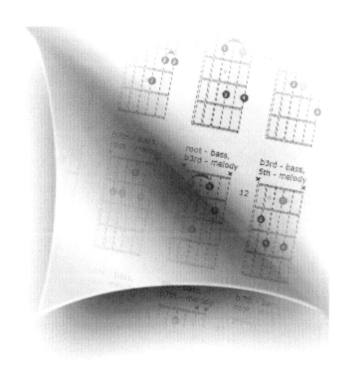

NOTES ABOUT LESSON 12

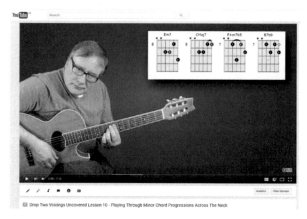

Drop Two Voicings Uncovered Lesson 10 - Playing Through Minor Chord Progressions Across The Neck

You will expand the ideas presented in the last lesson and build on previous ideas regarding substitution ideas. The lesson is split into two sections which is why the video covers two lessons.

Use backing track number 9 in conjunction with the chords that follow. Each chord gets four beats each.

YOUTUBE VIDEO

View the video "Playing Through Minor Chord Progressions Across The Neck" that accompanies Lesson 12 and 13 on Youtube at the following URL: www.youtube.com/watch?v=VLoKDa974e8

I - VI - II - V up the neck in E minor String Set 1 - 4

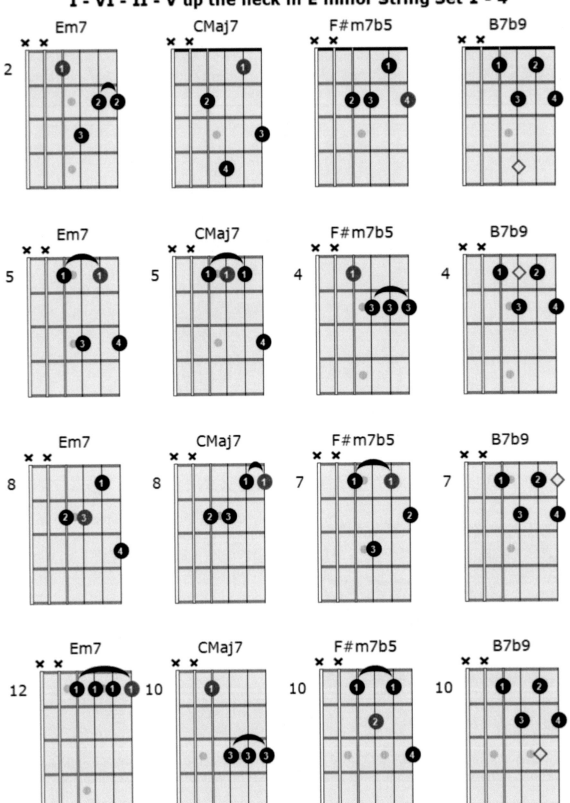

I - VI - II - V up the neck in A minor String Set 2 - 5

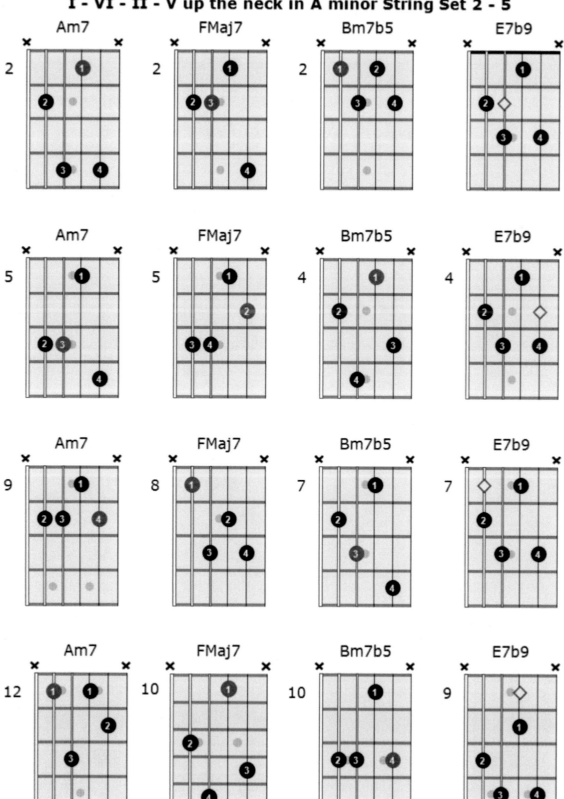

I - VI - II - V up the neck in C minor String Set 3 - 6

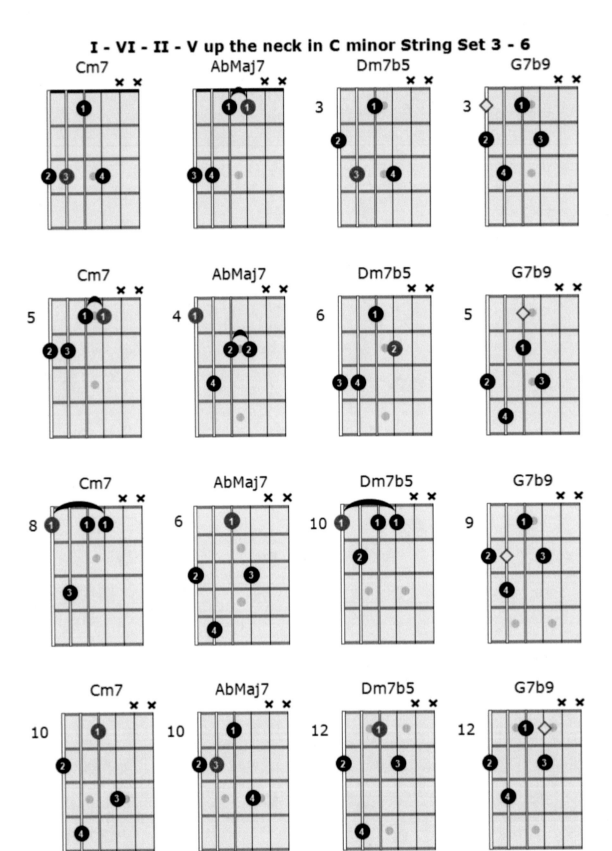

Lesson 13

Minor I - VI - II - V Progressions Across The Neck

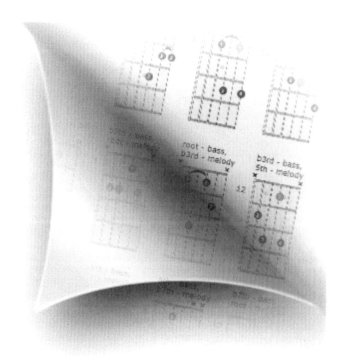

NOTES ABOUT LESSON 13

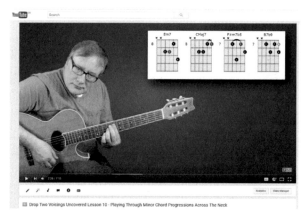

As mentioned in the last lesson's text, this lesson is actually viewed within the same video but what follows concerns the second half of the video. The chords that follow do not have a backing track. The ideas on the following pages cover playing right across the neck while outlining the I - VI - II - V progression. The chord progressions can be played in strict time or freely (rubato) as you wish.

YOUTUBE VIDEO

View the video "Playing Through Minor Chord Progressions Across The Neck" that accompanies Lesson 12 and 13 on Youtube at the following URL: www.youtube.com/watch?v=VLoKDa974e8

I - VI - II - V across the neck in F minor String Set 1 - 4

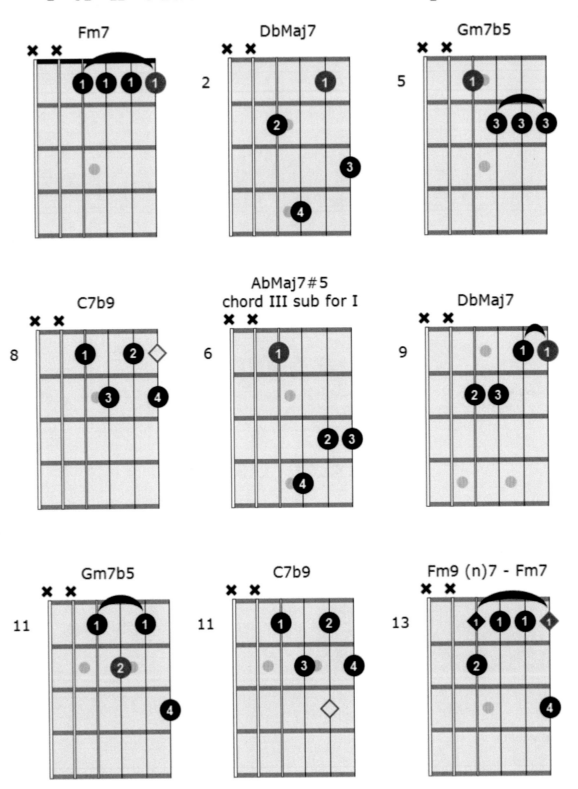

I - VI - II - V across the neck in A minor String Set 2 - 5

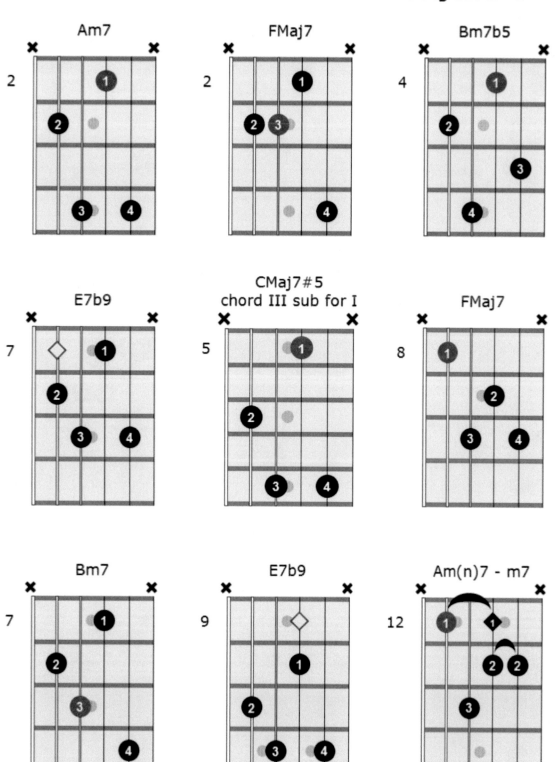

Am7

FMaj7

Bm7b5

E7b9

CMaj7#5
chord III sub for I

FMaj7

Bm7

E7b9

Am(n)7 - m7

I - VI - II - V across the neck in D minor String Set 3 - 6

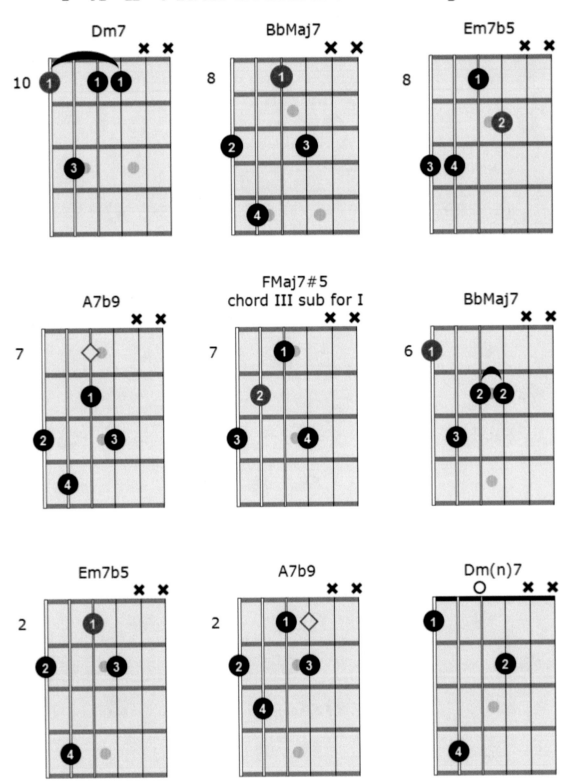

BACKING TRACK SONGS

There are three songs provided with backing tracks.

1. Funky G minor

2. Blues In A

3. Here You Go

Each song comes complete with music and tab so that you can learn the song as well as play the chords provided. Further, the backing tracks for the songs are provided in both slow and fast versions for you to practice up to the faster tempo if needed.

Finally, you will find additional pages of ideas in chordal form for all these backing tracks in the downloadable file which also includes the backing track mp3s to help you gain additional experience in "comping" over the progressions.

The "Here You Go" song is challenging and moves around a lot in terms of key centres.

PLAY ALONG

1. Funky G Minor

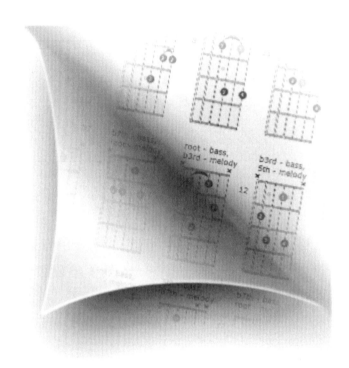

NOTES ABOUT FUNKY G MINOR

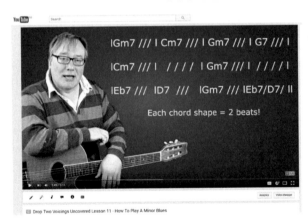

Drop Two Voicings Uncovered Lesson 11 - How To Play A Minor Blues

For me, this is where things really get interesting. This is where we put all the hard work to use by playing along with actual songs. These tracks have been written with one main objective; to give you a range of chord ideas that can be quickly slotted in to hundreds of songs that use the same or similar progression.

You should also learn to play the song as full music and TAB is provided, it would be great to hear some of you play these on Youtube! Remember to try out the alternative download progressions. If you have not done so already, please see page six for download instructions.

There are two backing tracks for you to work with called Funky G Minor; one at 84bpm and one at 104bpm once you're up to full speed.

YOUTUBE VIDEO

View the video "How To Play A Minor Blues" that accompanies this on Youtube at the following URL: www.youtube.com/watch?v=JcpodPzGaK4

Funky G minor
Use With The Guitar & Music Institute's "Drop Two Voicings Uncovered" volume 1 book

This music is part of the learning resources for the book "Drop Two Voicings Uncovered" and is not to be sold or used in any way other than as a learning resource. Please contact GMI if you wish to use the music other than as a learning aid.

Funky Blues in G minor page 1. Each chord gets two beats

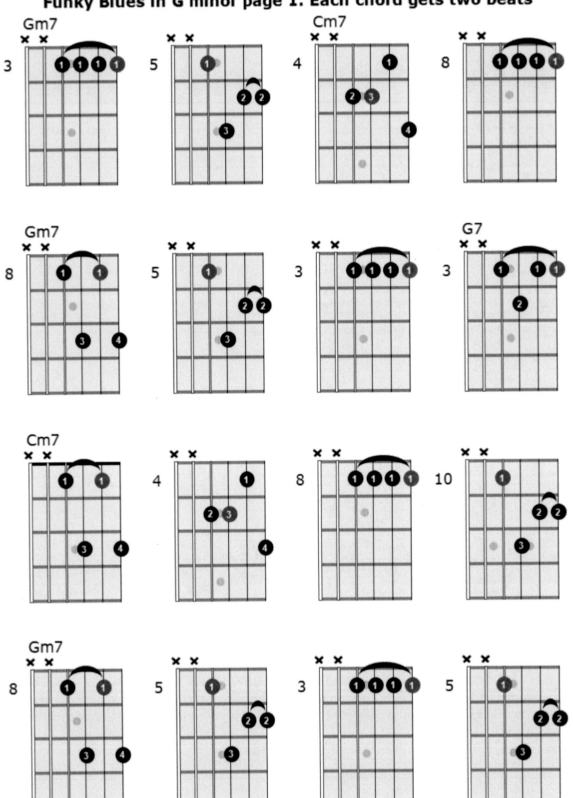

Funky Blues in G minor page 2. Each chord gets two beats

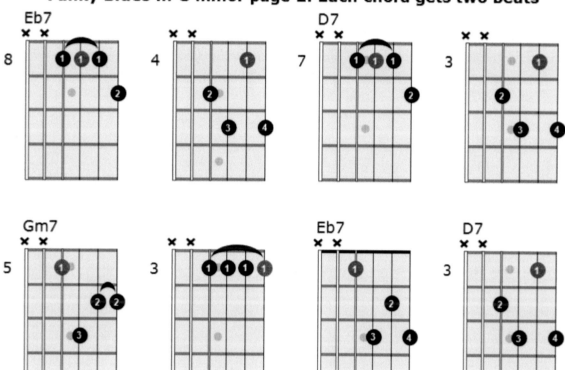

PLAY ALONG

2. Blues In A

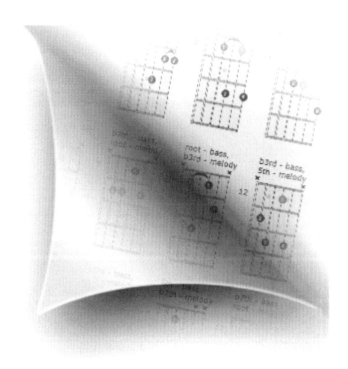

NOTES ABOUT BLUES IN A

As with the last play along, I wanted you to study a track based on a progression that you're probably going to already used in your playing experience. In this way, you will see chord ideas that you might never have considered before. Also, it's a jumping off point for your continuing work with blues progressions as you study the chord forms more. Finally, you can apply your best loved ideas into songs you already play regardless of key.

You should also learn the song as full music and TAB is provided. Remember to try out the alternative download progressions. If you have not done so already, please see page six for download instructions.

There are two backing tracks for you to work with called Blues In A; one at 78bpm and one at 116bpm once you're up to full speed.

YOUTUBE VIDEO

View the video "Chord Ideas For A Blues" that accompanies this lesson on Youtube at the following URL: www.youtube.com/watch?v=_6tg_EDFZow

Blues in A

Use With The Guitar & Music Institute's "Drop Two Voicings Uncovered" volume 1 book

This music is part of the learning resources for the book "Drop Two Voicings Uncovered" and is not to be sold or used in any way other than as a learning resource. Please contact GMI if you wish to use the music other than as a learning aid.

Blues in A page 1. Each chord gets two beats

A7
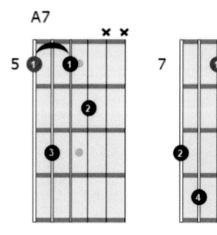

D7
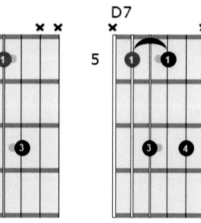

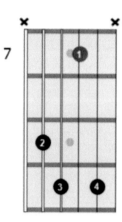

A7
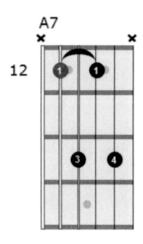

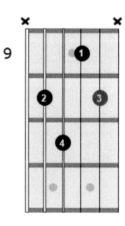

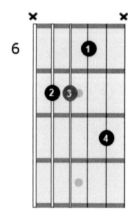

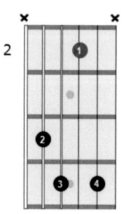

D7
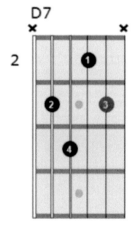

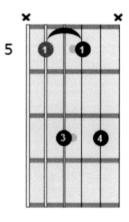

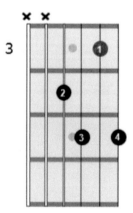

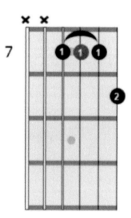

Blues in A page 2. Each chord gets two beats

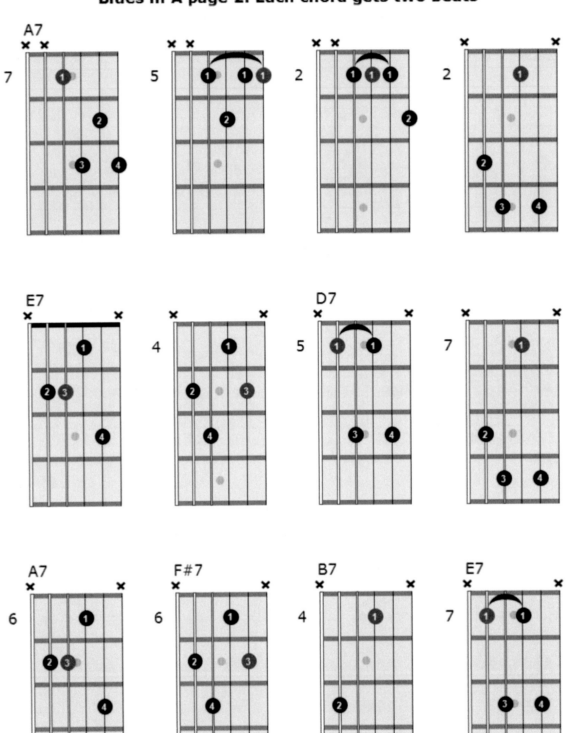

PLAY ALONG

3. Here You Go

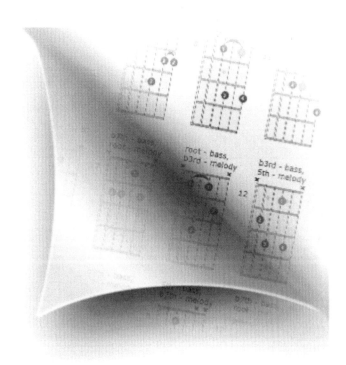

NOTES ABOUT HERE YOU GO

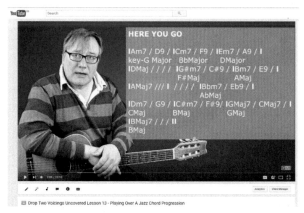

Here You Go is a challenging piece as outlined in the accompanying video to this lesson. Again, it's important that you watch this video as it explains the difficultly faced in playing through a song like this which is up tempo and harmonically complex.

Here You Go is really a marker for what will come in any further book created after this volume. I hope you enjoy it and really work hard to master it. Crucially, ensure that you understand the chords and their names. Don't just learn the changes without understanding what you are playing.

There are two backing tracks for you to work with titled Here You Go; one at 80bpm and one at 180bpm once you're up to full speed.

YOUTUBE VIDEO

View the video "Playing Over A Jazz Chord Progression" that accompanies this lesson on Youtube at the following URL: www.youtube.com/watch?v=DZiWXNBzoGg

Here You Go
Use With The Guitar & Music Institute's "Drop Two Voicings Uncovered" volume 1 book

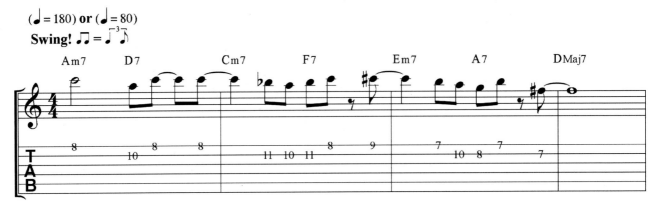

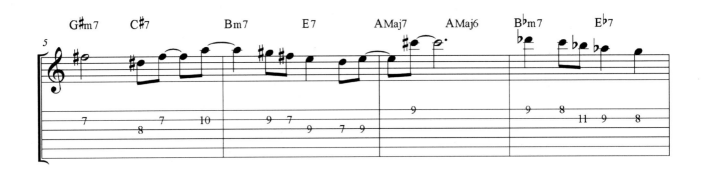

This music is part of the learning resources for the book "Drop Two Voicings Uncovered" and is not to be sold or used in any way other than as a learning resource. Please contact GMI if you wish to use the music other than as a learning aid.

Here You Go - two beats per chord string set 1 - 4 page 1

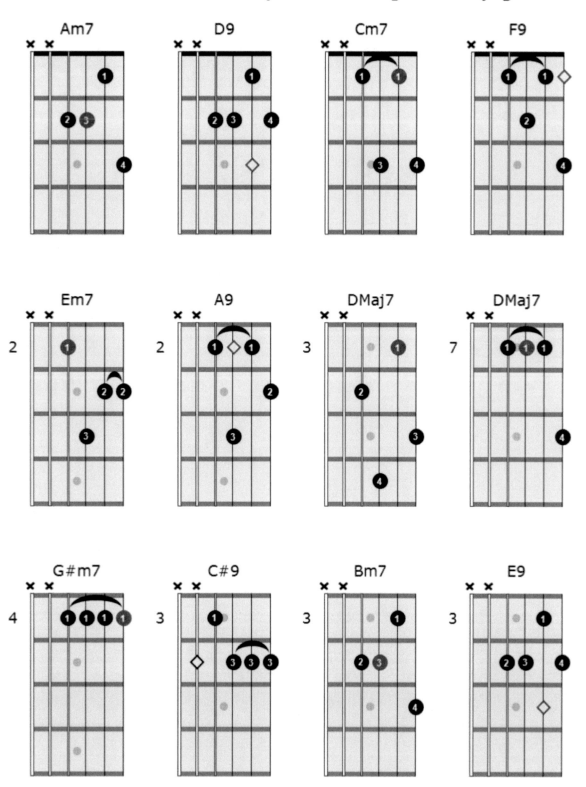

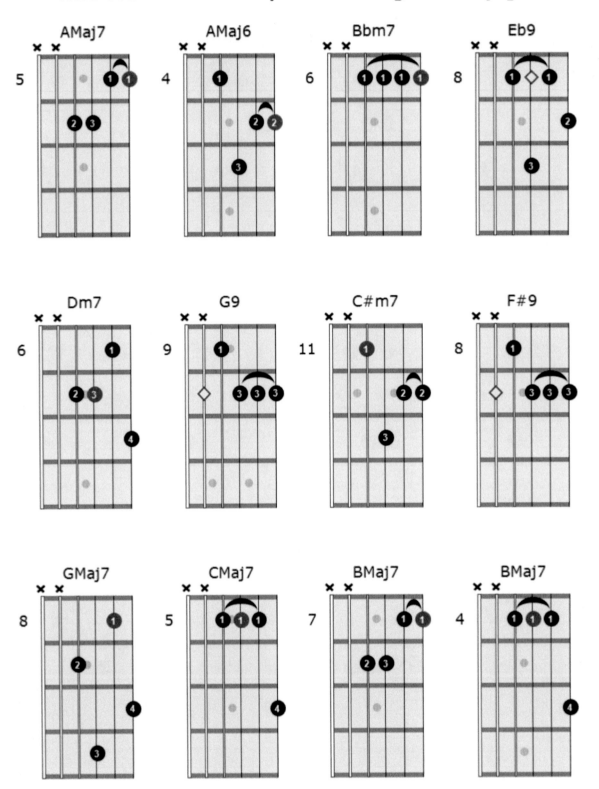

VIDEO LISTINGS

BACKING TRACK LISTINGS

FURTHER RESOURCES

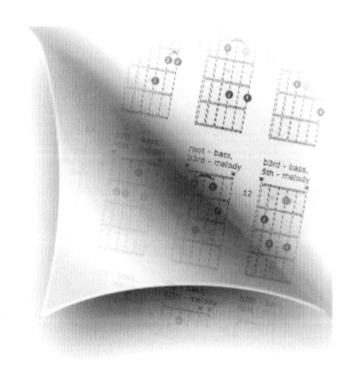

APPENDICES
AUDIO & VIDEO LISTINGS & FURTHER MATERIAL

The backing tracks (mp3) created for specific lessons are listed below. They are downloadable from the web address shown. To download these tracks (and all other materials offered in support of this book), you will be asked to input your first and last names and answer some questions relating to this book. This is done in an effort to decrease piracy. We created backing tracks with bass and drums only (apart from the songs at the end). This was done to help guitarists really listen to what is being played and stopped the guitar and keyboard sounds getting in the way of each other.

http://www.guitarandmusicinstitute/downloaddrop2voicings

AUDIO

1. LESSON 2 - Backing Track 1 minor Sevenths

2. LESSON 3 - Backing Track 2 Dominant Sevenths

3. LESSON 4 - Backing Track 3 Major Sevenths

4. LESSON 5 - Backing Track 4a II - V - I FMaj,AbMaj, BMaj, C#Maj

5. LESSON 5 - Backing Track 4b II - V - I AMaj, CMaj, EbMaj, GbMaj

6. LESSON 5 - Backing Track 4c II - V - I DbMaj, EMaj, GMaj, BbMaj

7. LESSON 7 - Backing Track 5a II - V - IMaj7- Maj6 Gmaj, BbMaj, C#Maj, EMaj

8. LESSON 7 - Backing Track 5b II - V - IMaj7- Maj6 Fmaj, AbMaj, BMaj, DMaj

9. LESSON 7 - Backing Track 5c II - V - IMaj7- Maj6 Cmaj, EbMaj, GbMaj, AMaj

10. LESSON 8 - Backing Track 6a I - VI - II - V in 6/8

11. LESSON 8 - Backing Track 6b I - VI - II - III - VI - II - V - I

12. LESSON 8 - Backing Track 6c I - VI - II - III - VI - II - V - I

13. LESSON 10 - Backing Track 7 I - VI - IV - V - III - VI - IV - V - I

14. LESSON 11 - Backing Track 8 minor II - V - I

15. LESSON 12 - Backing Track 9 minor I - VI - II - V

16. Funky Minor Blues Backing Track Slow 84bpm

17. Funky Minor Blues Backing Track Fast 104bpm

18. Blues In A Backing Track Slow 78bpm

19. Blues In A Backing Track Fast 116bpm

20. Here You Are Backing Track Slow 80bpm

21. Here You Are Backing Track Fast 180bpm

VIDEO

All of the videos created to accompany this book can be found in two separate places and offer slightly different approaches to learning:

1. Within the GMI website each of the videos are presented as individual blog posts. The blog posts offers elements already present in the book and shortened backing tracks for non book owners.

2. On the GMI Youtube channel. Go to YOUTUBE and search for "Guitar and Music Institute".

Once at the GMI Youtube channel go to the "PLAYLISTS" option on the GMI Youtube home page.

The GMI Youtube playlist that supports this book is titled "How To Play Advanced Chords - DROP TWO VOICINGS UNCOVERED". Please subscribe to our Youtube channel for further video updates.

VIDEO LIST WITH LESSON RELATIONSHIPS OUTLINED

Video Lesson 1 - Introduction To Guitar Drop Two Chords - Book: LESSON 1

Video Lesson 2 - How To Play Numerous Chords Over The Neck - Book: LESSONS 2, 3, 4

Video Lesson 3 - II - V - I Progression & Voice Leading - Book: LESSONS 5

Video Lesson 4 - Dominant Seventh To Dominant Ninth - Book: LESSONS 6

Video Lesson 5 - Chord Synonyms & Adding The Major Sixth Chord - Book: Lesson 7

Video Lesson 6 - Playing Up The Neck & Through A Chord Progression - Book: LESSONS 8

Video Lesson 7 - Understanding Major Diatonic Chord Harmony - Book: LESSONS 9

Video Lesson 8 - The I - VI - IV - V Progression & More! - Book: LESSONS 10

Video Lesson 9 - Minor Chord Scale Relationships Explained - Book: LESSONS 11

Video Lesson 10 - Playing Through Minor Chord Progressions Across The Neck - Book: LESSONS 12, 13

Video Lesson 11 - Funky G minor

Video Lesson 12 - Blues In A

Video Lesson 13 - Here You Go and final thoughts

FURTHER MATERIAL

You will receive within your extra download materials from the GMI website (see page six) the following additional material in PDF format:

1. Four pages of extra chord ideas for G minor Funky Blues.

2. Four pages of extra chord ideas for A Blues.

3. Four pages of extra chord ideas for Here You Go.

We will look at the possibility of producing and emailing out further materials to book owners once we have collated the feedback on Drop Two Voicings Uncovered.

FINAL THOUGHTS

When I was a teenager I went through a phase of buying guitar books. I would listen to my favourite guitar players and look for ways to emulate them. I would use any money I had to buy as many books on guitar playing, guitar players, technique, scales, chords as I possibly could. I'd sit on the bus home and look through the book from cover to cover, excited about the playing secrets this new book offered. I'd work through my new book for a week or so then my attention would wander.

As I grew a little older I started wondering what kind of guitar player I would be if I actually knew everything from every book I had ever bought, rather than just skimming material. I realised I was addicted to the new and was not learning enough from what I already had. From then on I started buying less and focusing more. If I did purchase a new book, I'd make sure it was going to really help me and that I learned as much as I could from it.

I want to encourage you to be honest with yourself and when you think you are done with this book, ask yourself "how much do I really know". Have you taken the chords into as many keys as you can? Can you confidently play along with all the backing tracks without a stumble and know the chords you are actually playing? Have you taken the ideas and concepts presented here, in the downloadable material and from the video series and applied it to other songs and musical situations?

If the answer to the last paragraph is yes, then well done and it will serve you well. If the answer is maybe, then perhaps it's time to go through everything one more time until it really sinks in.

I will be keeping a close eye on the feedback from everyone who gives it about this book. I intend to create a second volume which will build on the concepts presented here. It's up to people like you who purchase these materials to give feedback and guide me in the next volume. There are many things I could talk about and demonstrate but it's about ensuring a smooth learning path is created. Many are already written down, but there is space in this connected world for your thoughts and ideas to be thrown into the mix.

All the very best with your guitar playing and music making.

Ged Brockie

44512124R00066

Made in the USA
Middletown, DE
07 May 2019